STANDARD OIL
THE FIRST 125 YEARS

Wayne Henderson & Scott Benjamin

First published in 1996 by Motorbooks International Publishers & Wholesalers, 729 Prospect Avenue, PO Box 1, Osceola, WI 54020-0001 USA

Library of Congress Cataloging-in-Publication Data Available

ISBN 0-7603-0086-0

On the front cover: To millions of motorists, the red, white, and blue oval sign and crown-shaped gas pump globes epitomized gasoline and oil. This Standard station in Sayre, Oklahoma, carried Atlas automotive products, souvenirs, decals of the fifty states, and tourist supplies.

On the back cover: A sampling of collectibles from the Standard Oil family, clockwise from bottom: a 1935 Conoco Travel Bureau map of the United States, the famous Red Crown gas pump globe, and a collection of Mobil signs.

Printed in Hong Kong

CONTENTS

Introduction

Along West Market Street in Johnson City, Tennessee, a passing motorist may choose from numerous gasoline brands at fiercely competing stations. Approaching from the south is an abandoned Mobil location, followed by a company-owned and operated Conoco convenience store. Next in line is a Marathon location, currently being renovated. As you get closer into town, the motorists can drive into a car wash selling Pennzoil gasoline and into other convenience stores, branded Exxon, Chevron, BP, and Amoco. This juxtapositioning of brands is not unusual at all. Most cities of any size have gas stations from up to a dozen regional brands within their borders. Johnson City is unusual, though, in that the eight stations mentioned above sell products from eight of nine surviving gasoline brands that trace their origins to the inspiration, ambition, and yes, perhaps the greed of one man, John D. Rockefeller. Of the nine surviving Standard-related gasoline brands, only Arco, now found only in five far western states, is missing from the Johnson City gasoline market. If one were to travel north on Interstate 81 from Johnson City, through the Shenandoah Valley of Virginia, a motorist would eventually, in Pennsylvania, encounter stations that bear the Atlantic brand, forerunner to Arco and the true successor to Standard affiliate Atlantic Refining. When Arco withdrew from branded marketing in the East, the company sold off the former Atlantic marketing to an independent who logically branded the stations from Arco back to Atlantic. Although they are in the process of rebranding to Sunoco at present, Sun Oil having purchased the operation, some Atlantic stations remain, keeping representation of all nine surviving Standard brands in the East.

Marketplace gossip has long held that "all these brands are the same company, anyway." This book tells the story of how, 125 years after one man set out to control the petroleum industry, these companies have evolved from their government-enforced breakup to become fierce competitors, often involved in litigation among themselves, all the while cooperating on items ranging from trivial credit card exchange programs all the way to complex international ownership and control of petroleum exploration operations that dominate producer countries' internal politics and international position. In short, we are telling the story of Standard Oil.

While many works have been created on this subject, with production figures and refinery statistics reviewed and compared, this history differs in that this story is told through the perception of the companies the average consumer sees, those with retail presence in the marketplace. Next time you visit your corner convenience store, stop and realize that more than 125 years of international business operations, with a history that has changed the world in this century, is represented by the sign displayed overhead.

The Angel of Mercy, Early Years of the Standard Oil Company

Webster defines "standard" as "a unit by which all others are measured." We wish to tell the story of the unit by which all businesses, before or since, are measured. In short, we wish to tell the story of the Standard Oil Company. It is likely that had there been no Standard, that the entire history of the twentieth century would have been rewritten. For without the petroleum industry and its products, much of the twentieth century would have been vastly different. And without Standard, the petroleum industry would have never reached the levels of innovation that it did in such a short time. No doubt, the inventive spirit that led us through the industrial revolution and into this century was fueled and lubricated with petroleum.

Years have weathered the image, but this sign still identifies Standard service at Grainfield, Kansas.

But what of the product itself? Early man knew of petroleum and its uses as early as the days of Noah, when he was commanded by none other than God to build the ark, sealing it with pitch, which was nothing more than a petroleum-based asphalt substance found in seepage from the Earth's surface. Many thousands of years passed, though, before commercial recovery of petroleum was feasible. The search for a commercial product was driven simply by commercial applications—lighting and lubrication—and by man's greed. Stated simply, if enough money can be made, a method will be found.

Earliest oil production in commercial quantities was that which centered in the Oil Creek area of Pennsylvania in the 1840s. At that time, most illumination was fueled by animal and vegetable oils, and lubrication was also accomplished with products of similar origin. The Pennsylvania product was known as Seneca oil, or "rock oil," and was collected from the oil seepage and used primarily for medicinal purposes. Illumination needs had attracted the interest of the coal industry, which had developed the method by which oil was extracted from shale and refined as an illuminating fuel known as coal oil.

Experimentation in the mid-1850s led to the discovery that Seneca (or rock) oil and somewhat heavier deposits of asphaltic petroleum could be distilled into a superior lighting product that was named

One of the earliest Standard brand logos appears on this vintage 1917 globe. ***J. Sam McIntyre Collection***

"kerosene" in 1854. Development of this revolutionary new product was limited, however, by the availability of the raw materials necessary for its production. Collection of petroleum was limited to recovery of seepage and by skimming oil from the waters of oil-bearing creeks. No one knew just how to go about commercial recovery of petroleum. Salt drilling had produced some quantities of petroleum, and entrepreneurs of the day turned to drilling as a possible source of recovery for the greatly valued petroleum.

In the fall of 1857, a group of investors dispatched one of their own, Edwin Drake—quickly dubbed "Colonel Drake"—to a tiny village known as Titusville in the Oil Creek area of Pennsylvania. Most of a year and a half was consumed securing title to prospective oil lands and locating suitable excavation and drilling equipment and experienced operators. As the work progressed, money was ever in short supply as one by one the investors gave up and withdrew from the venture. In August 1859, nearly two years after his arrival in Titusville, crews working under the direction of Colonel Drake accomplished what many of the locals had said was impossible. They struck oil. Overnight speculators flocked to the scene, grabbing for every piece of available land and duplicating Drake's process. Storage and transportation problems arose quickly, and almost immediately overproduction, driven solely by ignorance and greed, very nearly destroyed the industry in its infancy.

Into production chaos came a young man from New York, who, along with a partner, became a broker in produce and virtually any other commodity that could be traded profitably. Discovering that there was money to be made with petroleum, the Cleveland, Ohio-based partners, John Rockefeller and Maurice Clark, eventually invested in a small refinery and began trading petroleum products on a commodity basis. In 1865, Rockefeller bought out his partner. Finding that more money could be made on refined products at retail than from crude or refined petroleum as a commodity, Rockefeller built another refinery and began concentrating on a growing trade in kerosene, both at home and abroad. In January 1870, in Cleveland, Rockefeller and several partners acquired along the way consolidated all of their holdings into a joint stock corporation known as Standard Oil.

The name "Standard" was chosen to represent their intent to market products of a known and consistent quality in an organized manner in a stabilized industry. Until that time, refined petroleum products varied greatly in quality and reliability and were produced, transported, refined, and marketed in a chaotic manner. Rockefeller and his partners soon discovered that the key to profitability in refining was to manipulate transportation methods and costs. To this end, arrangements were made with railroad operators to provide rebates and other kickbacks to Standard, reducing transportation costs far below published transportation rates. Standard, having guaranteed the railroads a minimum amount of freight daily, was able to secure this arrangement to the detriment of all other refiners in the area. As the other refiners fell one by one, Rockefeller and associates bought them outright or otherwise brought them into the fold.

Having conquered refining, Standard Oil faced off with the producers, who, without their own transportation and refining capacity, were at the mercy of Standard. Fighting back, producers in the Pennsylvania oil regions constructed a pipeline with connections to a railroad that was

Various Standard oil, grease, and water containers of the 1920s.

not affiliated with Standard. An engineering wonder, the pipeline carried crude over 100 miles to accessible rail facilities, where it traveled to new refineries along the coast. For a short time production companies had minimized Standard's grasp. Seeing the opportunity, though, Standard quickly constructed pipelines from the producing areas to major refining centers. No longer at the mercy of the railroads, Standard could purchase crude more advantageously and transport it directly to refining centers. Standard, in addition to refining, now controlled transportation.

Although this monopolization of petroleum did not escape the notice of government regulators and indictment by the public and press at that time, Standard's benefactors considered the company to be an "Angel of Mercy." In short, it had brought about an orderly industry from production, refining, transportation, and marketing chaos. The only thing held in contempt was the way this was accomplished. Rockefeller's methods, squeezing competitors until they either sold out to him or were forced out of business, were well documented in the news of the day. Yet Standard remained unscathed, primarily because each holding remained independent of the others, tied together only by common ownership of stock. That's right. Standard was still only a Cleveland-based refiner. However, Standard's owners, Rockefeller and associates, just happened to own hundreds of other companies that they directed to operate in association with Standard.

The Standard Oil Trust and Standard Oil (New Jersey)

A typical Standard station, still displaying crowns identifying Red Crown and Gold Crown gasolines at Sayre, Oklahoma, in 1961.

Nearly twelve years to the day after Standard was organized in Cleveland, the Standard Oil Trust was born. Created to unify its holdings and guarantee continuity in the event of the withdrawal of any of the partners, the trust was created to hold the ownership of the various divisions. Stock in the trust was held, in turn, by the founding partners. Management of the new concern, previously controlled at each company's headquarters, became more centered and directed by various operations committees. Day-to-day decisions, however, rested with the various divisions, some created and some acquired.

Many noted independent companies of that era had fallen into the Standard fold. Notable among them were Vacuum Oil Company, founded in 1866 in Rochester, New York, as a lubricants manufacturer; Atlantic Refining Company, also founded in 1866 in Philadelphia as a refiner; and Continental Oil, founded in Ogden, Utah, as an oil transporter and marketer in 1875. Each of these companies was a leader in its field, and as Standard expanded its grasp, they were natural additions to the Standard Oil Trust.

Among these leading independents, the first to come into the hands of Standard was Atlantic Refining. With a strong presence in Pennsylvania and a large refinery in Philadelphia, Atlantic was a logical move for Standard to make. Standard purchased Atlantic Refining in 1874 and continued to expand Atlantic's core business of Pennsylvania refining and marketing.

Next came Vacuum Oil. Vacuum was truly a lubricants pioneer, having developed a refining process utilizing a vacuum from which the company took its name. By the time Standard purchased Vacuum Oil in 1879, the lubricants heritage that would lead to Gargoyle Oils, later Gargoyle Mobiloil, was long established. Vacuum would thrive under Standard's control, becoming the premier supplier of lubricants to all Standard marketing operations worldwide. Vacuum's Gargoyle became one of the most recognized trademarks in the world.

Curbside Atlantic service in Pennsylvania about 1927.
R. V. Witherspoon

Continental Oil, having expanded throughout the West from a Denver, Colorado, base, was attractive to Standard because of its extensive marketing in the Rocky Mountain and Pacific Coast regions, areas where Standard was weakest. Continental, purchased by Standard in 1884, became one of the most independent-spirited of the Standard operations. With an expanded product line from the multiple Standard operations, Continental's reputation as a shrewd trader in petroleum products continued to grow, making the deal beneficial to all parties concerned.

The Standard Oil Trust had resisted entry into the risky business of oil exploration and production, preferring to profit from transportation, refining, and marketing, without which all of the production in the world would have been worthless. As Standard grew, however, it became ever more important to have sure sources of supply with which to operate its growing refinery capacity. The opportunity to become again an Angel of Mercy, this time in petroleum production, came in 1889 when Standard purchased the Ohio Oil Company. The Ohio, as it was commonly called, had been founded only two years before in the northwestern Ohio town of Lima by a consortium of oil producers from the area. Concentrating on oil exploration and production in the extensive Lima Field, The Ohio had rapidly become one of the most successful oil producers of that era. Standard, however, controlled the pipeline and rail transportation from the Lima Field to surrounding refineries, making Standard the primary buyer of Lima crude and allowing Standard to set prevailing purchase prices. Despite the constraints, The Ohio prospered, and this prosperity attracted the attention of Standard executives who had been dealing with the company. With the purchase of The Ohio, Standard now had a production base.

In addition to the acquisition of these major players in the industry, Standard had also extended its grasp by resorting to its tried and true method—controlling petroleum transportation. Various arrangements with the railroads and ownership of a growing network of pipelines gave Standard many advantages. Every method and means of oil transportation from the oil fields to the refineries was owned outright or controlled by Standard, effectively allowing them to control their purchase price and, in turn, the price of finished products. By the time Congress had passed the Sherman Anti-Trust Act in 1890, Standard had created a worldwide petroleum colossus, providing oil for illumination and lubrication to the world. Although Standard was a benevolent giant, keeping prices in reach of the common citizen, the Sherman Act was passed to protect independent businesses. As a result, the Standard Oil Trust ceased to exist in 1892. The assets were now in the possession of a new corporation, Standard Oil of New Jersey.

Standard Oil had taken advantage of New Jersey law allowing corporations domiciled there to own stock in other corporations. Other localities allowed only individuals to own stock in corporations. Thus the trustees who had held the stock in individual companies in trust for Standard Oil tendered their shares to Standard Oil Company of New Jersey. Each operation was streamlined to form some function within the larger picture of Standard of New Jersey. Among the companies and their assigned functions were: Standard Oil Company of New Jersey, domestic refining, eastern United States and foreign marketing; Standard Oil Company of Indiana, domestic refining and midwestern U.S. marketing; Standard Oil Company of Ohio, the original Standard Oil Company, was assigned domestic refining and marketing; Standard Oil Company

An early 1920s Standard Oil Company of New York station featuring its new Banner Gasoline.

of New York, administration; Atlantic Refining, production and refining; Vacuum Oil Company, lubricants manufacturing; Standard Oil Company of Iowa, western U.S. marketing; Continental Oil, Rocky Mountain production, refining and marketing; the Ohio Oil Company, South Penn Oil Company, and Prairie Oil and Gas, domestic oil production; Buckeye, Cumberland, Southern, Eureka, National Transit, and others, domestic pipeline transportation; and Union Tank Company, railroad transportation. Each depended upon the others, and together they functioned as a very effective competitor in the worldwide petroleum industry. Standard Oil was the largest corporation of any kind in America.

The Breakup of Standard Oil

The first governmental attack on Standard was, of course, the requirements set forth in the Sherman Anti-Trust Act that forced Rockefeller and his partners to dissolve the Standard Oil Trust, changing the corporate structure instead to that of a holding company, with Standard Oil of New Jersey owning the stock of each of the other operating divisions. While the new arrangement met the letter of the law, it was still in violation of the intent.

Following the establishment of Standard Oil of New Jersey as a holding company, Ohio was the first state to raise the issue of corporate monopoly practices. In 1898, the Ohio Justice Department began court proceedings to order those Standard divisions holding Ohio corporate charters to separate themselves from Standard Oil of New Jersey or face revocation of those charters. The action had been prompted by an independent refiner based in Marietta, Ohio, whose company had suffered at the hands of Standard. The Rockefeller influences in courts in Standard's original home state brought the lawsuit to a stalemate, and the action was terminated in 1902. The affected refiner, however, began pursuit of Standard in New Jersey courts and in federal courts, charging that Standard was violating the antitrust laws. This action was the one that eventually led to the breakup of Standard.

Early advertising thermometers promote Standard brands Red Crown and Polarine. ***Mike Douglass Collection***

Crowns have symbolized gasoline to motorists throughout this century. ***Mike Douglas Collection***

All was not litigation in the first decade of this century, though, as Standard was perfectly positioned to take advantage of the dawn of the automotive age. Early in this century, Standard branded its gasoline Special Red Crown, later shortened to simply Red Crown. The Red Crown brand, typical of the somewhat abstract trademarks of the era, was to be one of the properties of contention upon the breakup of Standard. The value of the recognized trademark was such that virtually all of the surviving marketing companies used it at one time or another. A variation was used by Standard of Kentucky, simply Crown, which together with Standard of Indiana's Red Crown brand, survived as active trademarks until 1961. Indiana Standard was perhaps the company most associated with the trademark, as their gas pumps topped with elaborately made cast milk glass crowns made the brand name Red Crown seem almost like a generic term for gasoline to three generations of midwestern motorists. Also introduced in this era was Standard's automotive motor oil, Polarine. The Polarine product was actually developed by Standard affiliate Atlantic Refining although all of the marketing companies used it for some time following the breakup of Standard. Polarine, too, survived until 1961, in use by both Standard of Indiana and Standard of Ohio until that time.

Also of note in the first decade of this century is that during this era Standard took the form with which we are most familiar, looking from a postdissolution point of view. By that we mean that the companies with which we are familiar today, including Standard Oil of New York, Standard Oil of California, even Standard of New Jersey, took on many of the functions that they would perform in the postdissolution era. This definition of function would, however, prove to be a source of frustration to many of the companies after the breakup. While Standard functioned well with each division performing its specific function, on their own the Standard siblings suffered from lack of integrated function. As a result, the divisions started their independent existence far behind the "new independents," such as Gulf and Texaco, in terms of self-sufficiency. The first decade beyond the breakup saw most of the companies in a grow or die position, helped only by the fact that they were connected to the great industrial colossus that had been Standard Oil.

Following the court actions in Ohio and New Jersey, the next significant legal attack on

Standard was put forth by the state of Missouri. In 1905, Standard was charged with violating antitrust laws by using the various operating companies doing business in Missouri, appearing as separate corporations rather than affiliated organizations, to fix prices and restrain competition from outside the trust. Despite repeated efforts by Standard executives to stall the investigation, the Missouri case was the first to show how Standard, through its various

Various Standard divisions and their interpretation of the Red Crown logo. Top row, from left: California, Indiana, Nebraska; center row: Ohio, Indiana, Nebraska; bottom row: Ohio, Indiana. ***Mike Douglass Collection***

An early Standard sales office, Canton, Ohio 1910.

faces to the public, worked to maintain an artificial price control of petroleum products, from wellhead to finished product. Also revealed was the complex ownership of the various entities, including how stock in the individual companies was being held in the names of executives of Standard of New Jersey for that company in an effort to hide the true ownership and control.

The Missouri action resulted in a court order that required the Standard operations in Missouri to be dissolved unless independence of the separate entities could be achieved. The affected divisions offered a countermeasure that included taking the state in as a partner in a new company to be formed from the Missouri properties in question. When this plan was rejected by the state, the Standard operations appealed the ouster from the state in a suit that would eventually be nullified by the breakup of Standard.

Also in 1905, neighboring Kansas took action against Standard for its part in dominating crude oil prices throughout the state. Using a tried-and-true method of control, independent operators attempting to ship their crude to non-Standard terminals or refineries or to points out of state were faced with unfavorable freight rates. Through much of its history, Standard had used the ploy of controlling transportation of crude oil or finished products to dominate the industry. Stated simply, a competitor's oil was worthless if they could not get it to market. Faced with antitrust action for the attempted control of Kansas crude, the Standard operating units in the state threatened to stop buying any Kansas crude, making the holdings of the independent operators that had raised the question essentially worthless, since Standard was still the dominant purchaser. Realizing that they couldn't sell to Standard, even at their price, and could not profitably ship to other potential purchasers, the independent operators gave in and withdrew their court action.

This action in Kansas and Missouri had not escaped the notice of the federal government, however, and an investigation was launched into Standard's potential violations of the Elkins Act, a congressional regulation of railroad rates and tariffs. The refined product shipments from Standard's Whiting, Indiana, refinery became the subject of the investigation. The investigation was to determine if Standard was offered and was accepting special freight rates from transportation companies for points between Whiting (considered an extension of Chicago) and East St. Louis. The question arose whether interstate (federally controlled) or intrastate (state controlled) freight rates applied since Whiting was, of course, in Indiana but was generally considered to be an extension of the Chicago yards and came under the jurisdiction of Illinois. In the end, Standard faced a fine in excess of $29 million, a record fine until that time, and the series of appeals lasted until the breakup of Standard.

The culmination of all these efforts came in a lawsuit filed in federal courts in St. Louis in 1906 charging that Standard, through use of its holding company arrangement, had conspired to violate the Sherman Anti-Trust Act of 1890, and had in fact continued to exist as a trust, in an effort to control the petroleum industry. More than three years of court action followed before Standard was found guilty of violating the Sherman Act in November 1909 and ordered to dissolve itself into more than thirty independent operating units. Appeals immediately went to the Supreme Court, which ruled in May 1911 that Standard would, within six months, be broken into thirty-four separate and distinct operating units, ownership of which would be distributed to stockholders proportionally. Such a dissolution seemed almost impossible within the time frame allowed, but by December 1911, stockholders of Standard Oil of New Jersey had received, in exchange for their holdings, proportionate amounts of stock in the thirty-four surviving companies. Executive talent was divided among the surviving companies, and each went its own way to the extent that the interlocking ownership would allow.

In retrospect, the breakup of Standard served mainly to strengthen the ability of the government to intrude into corporate affairs. Many people of the day, and those of us who can look on the situation with historical perspective, were against the breakup of Standard. Standard had maintained low prices for their products, in favor of the consumer; paid relatively high wages, in favor of its employees; and provided a constant return on investment, in favor if its stockholders. The company paid fair prices to independent producers from which they bought crude, provided constant business for the railroads for crude, and refined product transportation. If not a good corporate citizen, Standard had at least served as a stabilizing influence, indeed Rockefeller's Angel of Mercy, to the petroleum industry during its infancy.

The following companies are the thirty-four operating units set free in the 1911 dissolution of Standard. In the remaining portion of this book we will look at the nine Standard siblings that are most familiar to the public in that they are petroleum marketers whose signs and logos have appeared on service stations, representing branded gasoline, oils, and lubricants. Following the historical abstracts of the nine marketing companies, the final disposition of each of the thirty-four Standard siblings are listed.

The Standard companies and their primary function at the time of dissolution:

1. Standard Oil Company of New Jersey was assigned marketing in the mid-Atlantic region. Assigned to Standard of New Jersey were minor affiliates, Standard of Louisiana (marketing in the South), Carter Oil (production), Imperial Oil (Canadian operations), and Gilbert and Barker Manufacturing (production of service station equipment).

2. Standard Oil Company of New York was assigned marketing in New York and New England and held extensive overseas operations.

3. Standard Oil Company of Indiana was assigned refining and marketing in America's midwestern states.

4. Standard Oil Company of California was assigned production, refining, and marketing in the far West.

above and opposite
This early station signage promotes Red Crown and Polarine. ***Jack Heiman Collection***

5. Standard Oil Company of Ohio was assigned refining and marketing in Ohio.

6. The Ohio Oil Company was assigned production responsibilities in Ohio, Indiana, and Illinois.

7. The Atlantic Refining Company was assigned refining and marketing in Pennsylvania and Delaware.

8. Continental Oil Company, now Conoco, Inc., was assigned refining and marketing in the Rocky Mountain areas.

9. South Penn Oil Company was assigned production responsibility in the Pennsylvania oil regions.

10. Borne, Scrymser Company was assigned petrochemical business functions.

11. Cheesebrough Manufacturing was assigned production and distribution of medicinal petroleum products.

12. Washington Oil Company was assigned Pennsylvania oil production.

13. Union Tank Car Company was assigned responsibilities as a petroleum transportation firm.

14. Buckeye Pipe Line Company was assigned responsibilities as a common carrier pipeline today.

15. Vacuum Oil Company was assigned responsibilities as a lubricants manufacturer.

16. Standard Oil Company of Nebraska was assigned marketing responsibilities in Nebraska.

17. Standard Oil Company of Kansas was assigned production responsibilities in Kansas.

18. Standard Oil Company of Kentucky was assigned marketing responsibilities in the south central states.

19. Colonial Oil Company was assigned overseas production responsibilities.

20. Solar Refining was assigned refining responsibilities with one Ohio refinery.

21. Anglo-American Oil Company was assigned overseas operating responsibilities.

22. Waters Pierce Oil Company was assigned marketing responsibilities in Texas, Mexico, and the south central states.

23. Prairie Oil and Gas was assigned production and pipeline responsibilities.

24. Galena-Signal Oil Company was assigned responsibilities as a lubricants manufacturer.

25. Indiana Pipe Line was assigned responsibilities as a pipeline operator.

26. Northern Pipeline was assigned responsibilities as a pipeline operator.

27. New York Transit was assigned responsibilities as a pipeline operator.

28. South-West Pennsylvania Pipelines was assigned responsibilities as a pipeline operator.

29. National Transit was assigned responsibilities as a pipeline operator.

30. Eureka Pipe Line was assigned responsibilities as a pipeline operator.

31. Cumberland Pipe Line was assigned responsibilities as a pipeline operator.

32. Southern Pipeline was assigned responsibilities as a pipeline operator.

33. The Crescent Pipe Line was assigned responsibilities as a pipeline operator.

34. Swan and Finch was assigned responsibilities as a lubricants manufacturer.

Standard Oil Company of New Jersey-Exxon Corporation

The line drawing on this 1930 map accurately represents a typical Standard Esso station of the day.

By far the largest of the surviving Standard affiliates was Standard Oil of New Jersey, which we will simply refer to throughout the text as "Jersey." Taking advantage of liberal New Jersey corporate law, in 1892 Jersey became the holding company under which the entire Standard Oil Trust was operated. As such, it had the most dominating presence of any of the companies freed in the breakup. Yet despite its size, Jersey, primarily a refiner, was a crude-poor company, behind the proverbial eight ball right from the start in finding or buying a sufficient supply of crude to supply its refineries.

With the breakup of Standard, Jersey inherited as subsidiaries several small Standard divisions—specifically Standard Oil Company of Pennsylvania and Standard Oil Company of Louisiana—as well as the refinery at Bayonne, New Jersey, and rights to marketing using the various Standard trademarks in New Jersey, Maryland, Virginia, West Virginia, North Carolina, and South Carolina. Through its subsidiary, Standard Oil of Louisiana, marketing was also extended through Tennessee, Arkansas, and Louisiana under the brand name Stanocola, an image entirely different than that used in the Jersey territory. Jersey retained controlling interest of Canada's largest integrated oil

A typical early Standard dealer station, US 601 in Mt. Airy, North Carolina. *Thornton Beroth*

company, Imperial Oil, founded in 1880. With operations coast-to-coast in Canada, Imperial would prove to be a valuable asset in later years. Jersey also inherited much of the overseas marketing that the Standard Oil Trust had built in the preceding twenty years.

In the earliest years following the breakup, the Standard companies continued to interact in much the same way as they always had. In that regard, Jersey purchased much of its crude oil needs from the Ohio Oil Company, formerly Standard's production arm. Since the Standard divisions were somewhat autonomous in operation, independence created few differences in the day-to-day operation. Put simply, The Ohio found it and Jersey refined and marketed it. Even with the sure supply from The Ohio, Jersey continued to be strapped for enough crude to keep its refineries running and marketing demand fulfilled. Through another subsidiary, Carter Oil Company, Jersey began extensive exploration in the Midwest and Rocky Mountain areas. Through Carter, the Cushing, Oklahoma, oil fields were developed. Slowly, the greatest of all refiner/marketers was becoming more of a producer as well.

Gasoline marketing was only beginning to become an important part of Jersey's business at the time of the breakup. However, each year thereafter, gasoline for motor fuel use was becoming a more important product. Gasoline was distributed in bulk quantities to grocery and hardware stores, livery stables, blacksmith shops,

A vintage 1926 Standard station promoting new "Esso" at Johnson City, Tennessee.

Typical Standard "tank wagon" delivery truck, circa 1930. ***Larry Stancil***

and automobile dealers or service garages from conveniently placed bulk plants, usually one in every county. From these small facilities, commission agents courted the business of local retail merchants and distributed gasoline, kerosene, and lubricants to them for resale. In the earliest years, Jersey did not join in the attempt to establish company-owned and operated retail stations as other companies did but was content to continue as market leader in its territory with only minimal investment.

As automobile use became more commonplace throughout the Mid-Atlantic region, Standard's flanged signs were seen on more and more buildings, and "Standard Motor Gasoline" globes topped curb pumps in every city or town. These dealer-owned and operated outlets could be efficiently supplied from existing bulk facilities, and there was no shortage of station personnel as veterans returned from World War I, intent themselves on automobile ownership and its privileges. Products offered at these early stations were limited to Standard Motor Gasoline, Polarine Motor Oil, and several Standard greases. Special lubricants or other nonstock products could be ordered through the neighborhood dealer. The bulk plant commission agent for that area would deliver them along with his next scheduled delivery of fuel or lubricants.

Ever on the lookout for more dependable crude sources, Standard purchased a controlling interest in Houston, Texas-based Humble Oil and Refining in 1919. Humble, then only two years old, was primarily a production company with extensive production and pipeline properties in Texas and several small refineries in areas adjacent to producing fields. On the drawing board at the time of the purchase was Humble's Baytown refinery, which continues to be the backbone of Exxon's refining capabilities today. The Humble purchase was the first step toward Jersey becoming truly independent of its heritage. With oil flowing from Humble's wells through Humble's pipelines to Humble's and Jersey's refineries, Jersey was finally a vertically integrated company.

With crude oil sources secured, Jersey turned next to developing its marketing abilities. On the wholesale side, Jersey secured an agreement to supply Standard Oil of Kentucky virtually all of its product needs. Standard of Kentucky, which we'll call "Kyso," was assigned simply five-state marketing. With no oil wells, no pipelines, no refinery, but with numerous bulk sales facilities in Kentucky, Florida, Georgia, Alabama, and Mississippi, Kyso became essentially the world's largest gasoline jobber, buying more than 98 percent of its products from Jersey and reselling it throughout the South.

At retail, Jersey had resisted the temptation to blanket its sales territory with filling stations, as they were known, and continued to concentrate its sales efforts through an almost limitless number of independent dealers in their assigned territories. Marketing in the Standard of Louisiana territory paralleled that of the parent company, and dealers in those states proudly dispensed Stanocola products to motorists. In 1924, Jersey revised its marketing logo, introducing a bar and circle design with the name "Standard" prominently across the center. The new emblem not only appeared on dealer signage and pump globes throughout the Mid-Atlantic states but replaced the venerable Stanocola trademark in Tennessee, Arkansas, and Louisiana. The new logo was applied to an ever-growing number of company-owned Standard stations in the mid-Atlantic area. Independent marketers had been using equipment leases to tie independent dealers to their brand and to ensure exclusive representation. Jersey opted to go the other way, maintaining direct ownership and operation of hundreds of new stations in the mid-1920s.

Standard service in the 1930s, Main Street, Marshall, North Carolina.

A typical Esso station of the 1930s in preparation for reconstruction at Erwin, Tennessee, 1950. ***Chip Flohe***

Jersey, in conjunction with General Motors, formed the Ethyl Gasoline Corporation in August 1924. Ethyl, a trademarked brand name for tetraethyl lead-based antiknock additives for gasoline, had been the brainchild of General Motor's research labs in Dayton, Ohio. After initial marketing experimentation with several other companies, GM teamed with Jersey to produce the innovative additive. Globes indicating "Standard Ethyl Gasoline" appeared on pumps at Standard stations in ever-increasing numbers. Then, in March 1925, tragedy struck. Several employees of the Ethyl research and manufacturing facilities in New Jersey died from exposure to the chemical. Sales of "Ethylized" gasoline were suspended by the U.S. Surgeon General until studies could be made of the long-term effects. After more than a year of health-related studies, Ethyl was reintroduced to the markets on the condition that it be premixed at the terminals as opposed to the common practice of metering tetraethyl lead into gasoline directly at the retail pumps. Franchises for distribution rights to Ethyl gasoline were offered to qualified refiners and marketers, and many marketers quickly signed on. Jersey, having been a pioneer marketer of Ethyl gasoline, chose to re-enter the Ethyl market in 1926 with the introduction of a premium-grade Ethyl gasoline that would bear one of the world's best-known trademarks of all time: Esso.

In the most remote corners of the free world, Esso can be found alongside Coca-Cola and Kodak as symbols of America. In 1926, however, its use was limited to a brand name for Standard's Ethyl grade product. Esso is the phonetic spelling of the commonly used abbreviation S.O., for Standard Oil. Sales of the new product were immediately successful, as were sales for most Ethyl brands, and finally high-compression engines were possible since the chemists at Ethyl had eliminated engine knock, stemming from the wasteful, improper combustion of motor fuel.

Humble, too, had developed a retail presence in Texas. From a small number of owned and operated stations, Humble had expanded to encompass a branded network of dealers affiliated with Humble's local bulk plants. In the late 1920s, as highway development nurtured the growth of automobile use, Humble became an even larger figure in retail gasoline marketing, operating stations in most metropolitan areas and on major connecting highways between. Humble marketed a single gasoline grade, Humble Flashlight, but was quick to add an Ethyl grade when the opportunity was offered, renaming its regular grade Humble Flashlike and offering Humble Flashlike with Ethyl as a premium grade. Company and dealer stations alike reported excellent sales of the new products throughout Texas.

Jersey had expanded successfully into Pennsylvania, originally assigned to Atlantic Refining, using its Standard Oil Company of Pennsylvania subsidiary to establish wholesale and retail marketing throughout the state. Next in line were New York and New England, commonly called Soconyland from the primary gasoline marketer there. Indeed, Standard Oil Company of New York, Socony, had by the late 1920s become the dominant player in New York and New England markets. Jersey was poised to make the first major territorial move into competition with a former Standard sibling. The route chosen was through another Standard affiliate.

Founded in 1901 as the Standard affiliate and charged with miscellaneous overseas production and marketing, Colonial Oil Company had only recently become an industry presence in America with the 1928 merger with Boston, Massachusetts-based Beacon Oil. Beacon, a leading independent refiner-marketer, operated

An Essolube toy tanker truck of the 1930s.

Esso salt and pepper shakers manufactured during the 1950s.

Classic postwar Esso station, Knoxville, Tennessee. ***Chip Flohe***

an extensive network of filling stations in New England. With the merger, Beacon stations became Colonial Beacon stations and began to develop a new marketing innovation that would revolutionize the operation of filling stations. Colonial Beacon had discovered that motorists were predisposed to purchase other automotive products and services at the same location they purchased fuels and lubricants. The industry discovered through Colonial Beacon that filling stations could and should become "service stations," one-stop centers for automotive needs.

On the heels of the development of service stations, Jersey went shopping for a New England affiliate and returned with Colonial Beacon. In 1931, Colonial Beacon became a wholly owned subsidiary of Jersey, and with it a marketing presence was in place from the northern tip of Maine to the Gulf Coast of Louisiana. In nineteen states "Standard" gasoline, (Colonial in New England) was sold alongside the company's proudest product, Esso. So widely recognized was the trademark that in 1933 primary station identification was changed to the Esso brand. Stations became either Standard Esso Stations (Dealers) or Colonial Esso Stations (Dealers). A new logo, an oval with the Esso logotype across the center, appeared on stations throughout the nineteen-state marketing territory. The appropriate heading, Standard or Colonial, was still emblazoned across the upper field and "Station" or "Dealer," whichever was appropriate, across the lower. It would become one of the most repeated trademarks in history over the following forty years.

Jersey had, of course, marketed Vacuum lubricants in the earliest years as an independent, as well as motor oil bearing the famed Standard trademark Polarine. By the early 1920s, Polarine had become simply Standard Motor Oil. Just prior to the adaptation of the trademark Esso as Jersey's primary brand, Standard Motor Oil became Essolube Motor Oil. Then, in 1934, Jersey, through its lubricants subsidiary Pennsylvania Lubricants Company, introduced a temperature-stabilized winter motor oil they trademarked Uniflo. A summer counterpart, also called Uniflo, was offered in time for the spring oil change that year. Then, in 1935, Jersey combined the properties attributed to both in a year-round motor oil trademarked simply as Esso Motor Oil. Esso Motor Oil continued to be marketed until 1972.

Other marketing expansion was accomplished with the default of leading independents Tidewater Oil Company and Skelly Oil. Standard had extended credit to these leading independents in the early years of the Depression, and when they defaulted, Jersey acquired control of both, establishing Mission Corporation to operate these affiliates. From 1935 until 1937, they operated as Jersey subsidiaries, until speculator J. Paul Getty wrested control of Mission from Jersey. Next came Powerine. Denver-based Powerine was an established marketer in Colorado and had attracted the attention of Jersey. Controlling interest passed to Jersey in 1938, which operated Powerine as a semi-independent subsidiary until the end of World War II, when all of Jersey's western holdings were consolidated.

Chain store taxes in many states had forced all petroleum marketers to rethink their investment in service station ownership. Standard of Indiana reacted first when faced with enormous tax liability in Iowa. Stations were leased to independent dealers with long-term supply agreements tying the dealer to their supplier-landlord. Jersey faced a similar situation in West Virginia but escaped taxation through shrewd legal maneuvers. Seeing the light, stations were sold

A modern station for the highway era, Esso service in Oak Ridge, Tennessee, about 1955. *Chip Flohe*

or leased to independent dealers as quickly as possible, and "Dealer" identification plates were bolted over the word "Station" on Esso signs.

World War II, with its various hardships to the retail petroleum industry, proved nonetheless to be boom times for the industry in general. The Allied effort ran on oil, and Jersey was there to supply it. Lost in the war, however, were many overseas facilities, tankers, and valued personnel. Jersey had, by this time, established far-flung exploration and production facilities, in Europe, in Asia, and in the Middle East. While this book concentrates primarily on domestic development with a particular spotlight on marketing, it would be amiss not to include some tribute to those overseas Standard employees, from Jersey, Socal, and the others, who faced the tasks of war bravely. On the home front, Jersey expanded its western operation again during the war, purchasing Northwest Refining, of Cut Bank, Montana, marketers of Grizzly Gasoline in 1942. Immediately after the war, Jersey also

A gas pump globe promoting Esso aviation fuels.

purchased the marketing properties of Billings, Montana-based Yale Oil Company. Yale's stations, branded Litening, along with the Grizzly properties, were assigned to Jersey's production subsidiary, Carter Oil Company. Stations were rebranded Carter, using an oval logo identical to the Esso trademark then in use. The former

Bullet-riddled and rust-stained, this lonely Esso sign was still identifying a Virginia station in 1986.

Powerine stations also came under the Carter management, though for several years beginning in 1946 they were branded Oval-E. Their trademark, the Esso blue outline oval with a rounded "E" in the center, was like that used by Esso. Oval-E stations converted to Carter in 1950, ending the short life of one of the most unusual trademarks ever used in the petroleum industry. Carter signs appeared on stations from Minnesota to Washington and as far south as Kansas, creating an extensive marketing network deep in the heart of Standard of Indiana and Standard of California territory.

Jersey had, in 1935, attempted to enter the marketing area of Standard of Indiana. Three stations were opened in St. Louis, Missouri, under the Esso oval. Indiana sued, crying foul over the use of the Standard trademark Esso. As the Standard affiliate assigned to market in Missouri, Indiana controlled use of the Standard trademarks, including the abbreviation S.O. Since "Esso" was the phonetic spelling of that abbreviation, no differentiation could be made in radio advertising, and this marketing expansion generally served to confuse customers. Quickly losing to Indiana, Jersey closed the three stations in 1938. A precedent had been set with this action, and competition among the Standard companies would never be the same. Reaction to these three stations, and more than thirty years of lawsuits to follow, would ensure that all of the surviving Standard companies would eventually turn away from the historic Standard name.

In the years following World War II, with domestic gasoline marketing surpassing all estimates, Standard Oil Company of New Jersey consolidated all domestic marketing in the East into a newly formed subsidiary, Esso Standard Oil Company. Esso Standard concentrated on an ever-expanded retail presence, building new stations and securing leasee dealers as quickly as suitable sites could be located. In this building boom, the Chicago and Milwaukee markets were identified as possible expansion areas. To this end, Jersey again went shopping.

With the first purchase, Jersey claimed the number-one spot among Milwaukee gasoline marketers by purchasing Pate Oil Company in the spring of 1956. Pate, founded in 1933, marketed through nearly 150 dealer-operated stations in southeastern Wisconsin. Absorbed next, in the fall of 1956, was Chicago's leading discounter, Oklahoma Oil. Oklahoma, founded about 1935, had itself recently merged with cross-town rival Perfect Power. The purchase of Oklahoma placed Jersey into a position that it had never been in before, that of price marketer. Oklahoma operated about 150 high-volume salary-operated stations in the Chicago metropolitan area, selling gasoline for one or two cents below prevailing major brand prices. Jersey hardly had time to adjust to this new marketing concept when the opportunity to expand the Oklahoma operation arose. In the spring of 1958, Jersey's Oklahoma subsidiary purchased Indianapolis, Indiana-based Gaseteria, operator of 263 Bonded and Gaseteria stations in Indiana, Illinois, Iowa, and Kentucky. With the purchase of Gaseteria and conversion of the brand to Oklahoma, the Oklahoma operation developed a somewhat dual marketing style. While Oklahoma's original stations were all salary-operated discounters, luring customers with an established stamp-premium plan, many Gaseteria/Bonded stations were conventional dealer-operated outlets, creating an interesting mix of image problems in the marketplace.

One of the first steps taken by Jersey toward consolidating its marketing operations came with completion of the purchase of Humble Oil. While Jersey had controlled Humble since 1919, the remaining stock was not acquired until 1959. When the balance of stock was purchased, Humble's production and refining operations were merged with other Jersey-owned operations, and while the corporate name remained Standard Oil Company of New

Various Esso road maps, credit cards, and coloring books of the 1950s.

Standard of Louisiana was one of the Jersey affiliates. This pump globe promoted its products about 1920.

left
Assorted Stanocola signage 1916 to 1923. ***Mike Douglass Collection***

A collector's display of Esso marketing collectibles through the years. ***J. Sam McIntyre***

Jersey, the new Humble Oil and Refining was assigned all domestic petroleum marketing. Into the Humble fold came Esso Standard Oil, Carter Oil, Oklahoma Oil, Pate Oil, and the former Humble Oil stations. The corporate subsidiary name, Humble, was added to the station facades of each of these brands. Further enhancement of name recognition was accomplished by the introduction of the brand name Enco in 1960 to replace Oklahoma, Pate, and the remaining Gaseteria/Bonded stations. Enco was taken from Humble's new slogan "America's

A collection of Esso giveaways, toys, and products.

Leading Energy Company." Enco signs replaced Carter and Humble signs the following year, with Esso remaining in those nineteen states where it was allowed.

In another expansion move into new territory, Humble Oil and Refining purchased Columbus, Ohio-based Sun Flash Oil. Sun Flash, dating back to 1935, operated about thirty high-volume stations in central Ohio. When Humble attempted to brand these stations Esso, Standard Oil of Ohio objected on the grounds that the Sohio stations had marketed Esso motor oils, supplied by Jersey, for nearly thirty years and had built up an excellent reputation associated with the name. Sohio also objected to the use of Enco, being of similar appearance to Esso, so Humble opted to rebrand their Ohio stations Humble. As Humble signs came down in Texas, new Humble signs in a rounder oval design were being installed in Ohio.

In the midst of this expansion, though, came disappointment on the wholesale marketing side. In 1961, Standard Oil of Kentucky, operators of "Standard Oil" stations in five southeast states, was purchased outright by Standard Oil Company of California. Kyso, as indicated earlier, was almost totally dependent upon Jersey for products. With the purchase, Socal moved quickly to phase out Jersey's supply agreements with Kyso. As a result, Humble mounted an increased effort to buy or build its way into Kyso territory, where Esso products already had an excellent reputation having been sold by Kyso. Georgia and Florida were targeted first, and chains of private brand stations were purchased

A modern Exxon outlet, Asheville, North Carolina.

Standard in quotation marks always refers to the Jersey company. This globe identifies Standard products in 1923. ***J. Sam McIntyre Collection***

and converted to Esso in record numbers over the next several years. Socal sued over the use of the Esso name, however, and after a lengthy court battle, Esso stations in the five former Kyso states were rebranded Enco in 1967.

Further modernization of Humble's marketing image came about with a 1965 reimaging, including a revision of the trademark ovals. The brand names Esso, Enco, and Humble were placed inside a wider, light blue oval outline, replacing the thin dark blue outline in use for thirty-two years. Stations, too, received a reimaging, with red panels, interrupted by a white field with the appropriate oval logo, replacing the red stripes that had adorned them since the end of World War II. Gas pumps were reimaged, with white becoming a more dominant color. The entire image appeared somewhat European and served to further enhance the Humble brands in their respective marketing areas. California, so dependent on automobile travel that it could claim to be the world's largest gasoline market, was next on the list. Humble had purchased several small chains in California in the early 1960s and had attempted to purchase the former Tidewater Oil marketing throughout their former Associated Oil Company territory. When the purchase was thwarted in the courts, Humble withdrew, but in 1967 was allowed to purchase the former Signal marketing from Socal. With this purchase, Enco signs went up all over California.

When Socal prevailed over Jersey in the 1967 court ruling over the use of Esso in the Southeast, Jersey, through Humble, began searching for a new identity, something not so far removed from the prevailing trademarks and image, but nonetheless a trademark that could be used nationwide. Enco was considered and then discarded when it was revealed that the word had some undesirable connotations in several foreign languages. A computerized search was made of letter combinations worldwide to produce a word that had no meaning in any language. After a four-year search, the word Exxon was selected. Two logos, one rectangular and one oval, were designed, and stations in Athens, Georgia; Battle Creek, Michigan; Manchester, New Hampshire; Nacogdoches, Texas; San Luis Obispo, California; and Zanesville, Ohio, were temporarily reimaged with the new logos. In 1972, the rectangular logo was chosen, and Exxon signs replaced Esso, Enco, and Humble signs nationwide. By early 1973, the most expensive name change in history was complete.

The conversion to Exxon came just in time to see the nation through its worst energy crisis since World War II. With disruption among Middle Eastern oil producers, whom Jersey and others had been dependent upon since after World War II, crude supply shortages forced refinery slowdowns and long lines at the gasoline pumps. Conservation became a household word overnight, and Exxon channeled its advertising toward this public-spirited response to the crisis. Another shortage, triggered in 1978 by other Middle East developments, forced gasoline prices over $1 per gallon and witnessed the closing of thousands of stations. Marketers withdrew from areas where they could no longer compete profitably. Self-service, barely a footnote on sales charts before 1970, was embraced by petroleum marketers as a cost-cutting measure. Many Exxon

This globe was used by a European affiliate of Standard of New Jersey. The Esso brand is known around the world.

dealers operated "split-island" stations, with one full-service and one self-service island and gasoline prices on two levels, accordingly. Exxon was not immune from other marketing cutbacks, and the 1980s saw a greatly reduced marketing area. The 1980s also took Exxon from being an automotive services retailer to a consumer-oriented retailer as convenience stores swept the country. Originating with Dallas, Texas-based Southland (Seven-Eleven) and with Minneapolis, Minnesota-based Erickson (Holiday, SuperAmerica), convenience stores swept across the country in the early 1980s, as hundreds of abandoned service station properties were reopened as convenience stores. Exxon, having sold many company-owned commission-operated bulk plants to independent jobbers in the 1960s and 1970s, found an extensive market in the convenience store boom as hundreds of Exxon-branded jobbers replaced stations with stores.

With more than $87 billion in assets, today Exxon ranks number one in assets and net income among all oil companies and brands nearly 9,000 outlets in thirty-seven states. The Exxon brand has reappeared in Kentucky and Ohio but has all but disappeared from most of the Midwest. Stations were reimaged again in the late 1980s, and today's Exxon outlet is truly a consumer-driven convenience outlet for motor fuels.

above and right
Esso products and giveaways of the 1960s.

A Humble Handy Oil can from 1961.

Typical Esso oil cans of the 1960s.

Collection of early Esso motor oil cans.

These cans are similar in design to Esso oil cans, but they all bear the identification of one of the Esso affiliate brands.

Standard Oil Company of New York-Mobil Corporation

In 1934, Socony-Vacuum was still using the Socony brand name on products sold in its original territory. This contrasts with the 1934 White Star Mobilgas map that shows the transition between the old White star brand and image and the new Mobilgas image.

The Standard Oil Company of New York, better known by its cable address acronym "SOCONY," was created in 1882 as the administrative division of the Standard Oil Trust, maintaining the various financial and office functions for the entire operation. In the 1890s, Socony ventured into refining and marketing, primarily for export. Soon, Socony kerosene was known throughout Asia, and Socony developed an inexpensive lamp for its use, bringing modern illumination to the Orient. With the breakup of Standard, Socony was left without crude reserves of any kind and was forced to buy on the open market, primarily from Standard siblings The Ohio, Waters-Pierce, and South Penn. Socony had emerged from the breakup of Standard Oil in much the same situation that Standard of New Jersey was in. Standard had functioned well as a complex industrial machine, each operation complementing the others well. Independently, though, the companies did not fair so well, as is evidenced by the actions of Standard of New York, or Socony, as it was known. With an extensive marketing network already in place, both in the northeastern United States and in Asia, the company had little choice but to seek out the crude to refine and sell.

Socony began branded gasoline marketing in New York and New England in 1915, a natural extension of the bulk facilities already in place. Prior to this time, some gasoline marketing had been attempted through regional jobbers, but lacking consistent supply, an extensive jobber network was not feasible. Instead, independent dealers were solicited, and soon the Socony shield logo was known in every village and town in Socony territory. To ensure a constant supply of crude oil to refine and sell, Socony purchased a minority interest in Dallas,

Magnolia was Socony's Texas affiliate. Shown here is an early Magnolia sign.

Texas-based Magnolia Petroleum. Primarily a production company, Magnolia was well endowed with crude oil, having developed the Corsicana, Texas, oil fields. Magnolia was founded in Corsicana in 1894, and by the time Socony purchased a minority interest in 1918, it was already a fully integrated oil company. The Socony-Magnolia merger was very successful, giving Socony access to crude and Magnolia sources of refined products to sell. Seven years later, Socony acquired the balance of Magnolia, making it a wholly owned subsidiary.

Such was the success of the Socony-Magnolia merger that in 1926 Socony went looking for potential partners in a West Coast venture. General Petroleum was chosen. Founded in 1910, General was a pioneer in the California oil fields, had developed a refinery at Vernon, California, and was involved in marketing refined products all along the Pacific Coasts in North and South America. In a sense Socony

An early White Eagle-branded Ford dealership.

was merging with operations somewhat more self-sufficient than its own, giving the new entities access to capital for expansion.

No doubt Socony was studying the map, particularly the marketing territories map, when negotiating mergers. Next in line came White Eagle Oil and Refining, based in Kansas City, Missouri. White Eagle was founded in 1916 as a production company and operated three strategically located refineries, ideally suited to supply refined products to a network of bulk plants and filling stations across the Midwest. Socony purchased White Eagle in 1930. While crude production and refining capacity was of utmost importance to Socony, these three mergers significantly increased Socony-affiliated gasoline marketing, essentially from coast to coast. The various entities retained their identity, both in operation as subsidiary companies and at the gas pump, where Socony, Magnolia, General, and White Eagle trademarks were still proudly displayed. Despite the success, Socony's next merger would prove to be the most significant.

Vacuum Oil Works was founded in 1866 in Rochester, New York, as a lubricants refiner. The company's earliest products, kerosene and various lubricants, were distilled by a special process using a vacuum, hence the unusual name. By 1879, when Standard purchased Vacuum Oil, Vacuum was the largest producer of branded lubricants in the world. In the Standard era, Vacuum's oils were marketed under the Gargoyle brand name, and among its most famous products was a superior oil for the new gasoline engines coming into everyday use. The new product, introduced about 1904, was called Gargoyle Mobiloil.

Standard's status as a truly integrated operation was greatly enhanced by the Gargoyle products. Virtually every one of the Standard marketing divisions sold the Gargoyle oils. When Standard broke up in 1911, Vacuum emerged in a somewhat unusual position of having an excellent product manufactured through excellent facilities, with virtually no sales department to market the product. While most of the Standard

left
Perhaps the most beautiful gas pump globe ever created, the White Eagle stood tall, identifying gasoline to midwestern motorists.

siblings scrambled for crude, Vacuum scrambled to get market exposure. Fortunately, since most of the former siblings were without a premier lubricants line, they continued to purchase Vacuum's products, marketing them all over the world. As a marketing department was developed, many independent gasoline marketers, garages, and other oil companies were signed on to the Mobiloil program. Gargoyle Mobiloil signs were probably one of the most common sights along the nation's roadsides from 1911 until 1930.

By the middle 1920s, Vacuum had expanded into gasoline marketing in Ohio, Pennsylvania, and in the Chicago area, under the Mobilgas brand name. In the '20s, the Mobilgas brand was always closely identified with the corporate name Vacuum Oil. In 1929, Vacuum Oil purchased St. Louis-based Lubrite Refining Company, a company that was primarily a lubricants refiner but operated gasoline

A typical neighborhood Mobil station from the 1950s, Memphis, Tennessee. *Chip Flohe*

This classic Mobil station stands at Goochland, Virginia.

stations in Missouri, Iowa, Illinois, and Indiana. Use of the Lubrite name continued, although the gasoline sold carried the Mobilgas brand, almost as if it was a franchise. Vacuum Oil's Mobilgas was now available from the Atlantic Coast all the way to Iowa. Not content to rest with the success of this expansion, Vacuum began negotiations to purchase an even larger marketer.

Milwaukee-based Wadhams Oil Company was founded in the 1870s as a specialty lubricants marketer and by 1915 had begun building up a network of gasoline stations throughout Wisconsin, Minnesota, and in the Chicago area. A flamboyant marketer, Wadhams constructed stations resembling Chinese pagodas throughout its area, various sizes designed for the particular demographics. In 1929, Wadhams purchased its largest independent competitor, Milwaukee neighbor Bartles McGuire Oil Company. With the addition of the former Bartles Bonded stations, Wadhams was a leading marketer in Wisconsin and an early proponent of the "Red Hat" association, the Independent Oil Men of America (IOMA). Vacuum Oil had landed a big one with the 1930 purchase of Wadhams. Wadhams continued as a semi-independent subsidiary, although Mobilgas branding began to appear alongside the Wadhams brand.

To further solidify its position in America's industrial upper Midwest, Vacuum Oil went shopping again, this time in Detroit. Purchased in 1930, Detroit-based White Star Refining Company added more than 1,500 stations to the Vacuum Oil Mobilgas marketing in Ohio, Indiana, and Michigan. White Star was a well-established brand, and again, the Mobilgas name was added alongside White Star, almost as if Mobilgas was a franchise product.

As 1931 dawned, both Socony and Vacuum were independently successful Standard siblings, having overcome the early obstacles to become two of America's most successful oil companies. Socony was a motor fuels marketer, while

The award-winning Mobil "Pegasus" station design was introduced in 1964. This example was built outside Mocksville, North Carolina, in 1968.

Vacuum was a lubricants manufacturer that just happened to have a solid position in gasoline marketing using a trademark tied to its successful lubricants line. Court approval was necessary, but in 1931 these two successful siblings reunited to form Socony-Vacuum Oil Company.

Since both Socony and Vacuum were the products of many mergers and acquisitions, no uniform image existed from region to region within the company. The merger only added to this somewhat confused marketplace presence. Vacuum had used the Mobilgas brand almost as if it were a franchise or a licensed product such as Ethyl. Socony had never even standardized this much, and its affiliate stations retained their original brand and images. With the merger, however, the new entity became determined to take advantage of its nationwide presence with a single national identity. Vacuum's Mobilgas brand name was the best known of all of the brand names in use, primarily because of its ties to Mobiloil. Socony had several foreign subsidiaries that used a Pegasus design to symbolize speed and power, attributes certainly desirable to petroleum products. By 1934, it was decided to tie the Mobilgas brand to the Socony Pegasus for a unified image nationwide. Those affiliates wishing to retain some identity could continue to display the subsidiary name in a secondary position across the bottom of the shield logo chosen, a design adapted from that used by Socony from its beginnings in gasoline. Soon, Mobilgas-Wadhams or Mobilgas-White Star (logo only) shields appeared as station identification throughout the respective territories. Regional gasoline brand names were abandoned in 1934 in favor of Mobilgas (regular) and Mobilgas Ethyl (premium), renamed Mobilgas Special in 1936.

Despite this unity, merger fever had not left the new company. The search remained for marketing companies that would solidify Socony's position in those areas where the company

The classic Socony shield logo appears on this pump globe from before 1920.

already had supply and distribution facilities. To this end, in 1934, the newly united Socony-Vacuum purchased two regional marketers, Independent Oil of Altoona, Pennsylvania, and Metro Oil of Jamestown, New York. Metro had been affiliated with Socony for a long time, as it was an early wholesale distributor of Socony products. The Metro name was preserved as Socony-Vacuum's brand name for motor grade gasoline as late as 1955.

Socony-Vacuum's White Star division had long marketed a special motor fuel they called Staroline. Shown here is a pump globe from the late 1920s.

Further expansion on the West Coast was accomplished with the 1940 purchase of controlling interest in California's most image conscious marketer, Gilmore Oil Company. Gilmore was nothing short of a flamboyant marketing company, an early sponsor of automobile racing, and an excellent addition, through the General Petroleum subsidiary, to Mobilgas marketing. World War II interrupted before Gilmore stations could be completely reimaged, but by the end of 1945, the Red Lion had jumped off into the western sunset, chased away by Socony-Vacuum's Flying Red Horse.

The end of World War II marked the beginning of the modern era of Socony-Vacuum's marketing. The various regional images were

Socony's premium gasoline from the early 1920s was branded "Aviation," typical for the era.

eliminated, and Mobilgas and Mobiloil became two of America's most recognized trademarks. The Mobilgas shield appeared across the country, in all states except those in the deep South. Always on the leading edge of marketing images, the famed Mobil flying horse leapt in porcelain and neon across station facades, on rooftops, on signs and pumps. With the advent of plastic signage, Mobil was the first company to avail itself of 1950s image studies and recreated its logo to better accommodate the new material. The new elongated shield was introduced in 1955, gradually replacing the classic shield by 1958, although the Mobilgas and Mobilgas Special gasoline brands remained in use until 1962, when they were replaced with Mobil Regular and Mobil Premium, which used the new logo in advertising. Stations were reimaged as well, with blue becoming a more dominant color in station design.

In the early 1960s, Mobil became a participant in the Keep America Beautiful campaign, designing a station that could be built in harmony with surroundings in suburban neighborhoods. Known as the "Pegasus," the station prototype was unveiled in 1964. Featuring round pump island canopies standing like mushrooms over polished stainless steel cylindrical pumps, the Pegasus was a significant departure from Mobil station designs in use up until that time. Natural color brick and wood, even stone, were selected as building materials. Along with the Shell "rancher," Mobil's new design led the way in the beautification of the service station in the 1960s.

Socony Mobil Oil Company, the corporate name adopted in 1955, became simply Mobil Oil Company in 1966. A new logo was introduced with the new name, with Mobil lettering in blue except for the "o," which was in red. Design awards were again bestowed on Mobil, as the new logos went up as station signage at Pegasus-style stations nationwide. The famed flying horse was relocated to a lesser position of prominence, appearing on illuminated discs on station building signage. With the reimaging, the flying horse appeared on a white disc wherever used, on tank trucks, in print. Gray became a more prominent color in marketing image as well, a trend all of Mobil's competitors would follow more than twenty years later.

Vacuum introduced the Mobiloil trademark more than twenty years before the Mobilgas brand appeared. This early globe shows Vacuum's earliest use of the brand.

Mobil pump signs from the 1960s.

The gas shortage years of the 1970s saw Mobil diversify with the purchase of Marcor, parent organization of Montgomery Ward and Container Corporation of America. Suddenly an oil company was a major retailer as well. Government attacks on the petroleum industry were countered by Mobil advertising, a practice Mobil continues to the present. In the late 1970s, Mobil began conversion of some unprofitable company-owned locations into self-serve, convenience store Reelo and Sello stations. The experiment with convenience stores and their secondary brands opened the doors to branded Mobil involvement. Today more than 2,000 of Mobil's 7,000-plus stations are company direct-operated convenience stores. Many of the other 5,000 or so Mobil outlets are jobber-operated convenience stores as well. Always a lubricants

A collector's display of Mobil memorabilia. The petroleum collectibles hobby offers many varied specialties for the enthusiast.

Mobil motor oil cans from the 1930s through the 1960s.

leader, Mobil was also a pioneer in this field as well, with Mobil 1 being the first widely marketed synthetic motor oil when it was introduced in 1975.

Mobil today ranks number two in assets behind Exxon, with more than $40 billion in assets today. Mobil sold the Marcor interests in the 1980s to concentrate on the company's core businesses in energy production. Mobil's Flying Red Horse is certainly one of the world's most widely recognized trademarks, identifying Mobil products worldwide.

These motor oil cans date from after the introduction of the "red o" logo in 1966.

Standard Oil Company of Indiana–Amoco Corporation

The great refinery at Whiting, Indiana, is today a massive complex that stands as a monument to the great twentieth century industrial colossus. From its creation in 1889, Standard Oil of Indiana has been a manufacturer, taking raw materials (crude oil) through the refining process to create a wide array of finished products. The most "Standard" of the Standard affiliates, its torch and oval signs still read "Standard" at many stations throughout thirteen states of the company's marketing territory.

Standard of Indiana, which we will refer to simply as Standard in this text, emerged from the breakup of Standard with possession of the huge Whiting, Indiana, refinery complex, refineries at Wood River and Sugar Creek, Illinois, and domestic marketing in Indiana, Illinois, Wisconsin, Minnesota, Iowa, North Dakota, South Dakota, Kansas, and Oklahoma. In the 1890s, Standard had established hundreds of bulk plants throughout the territory and had tank wagon drivers on established sales routes serving the growing agricultural industry's needs. The sales routes were the nation's first rural free delivery offered by any company in the country. The breakup of Standard corresponded to the rise in automobile

Although by 1949 most Standard stations were given a new image that included the new torch-and-oval logo, maps from that year still display both logos in a transitional scene.

above
One of the earliest branded gas pump globes, this oval glass Red Crown globe dates from about 1915 to 1916.

right
Nothing says it better. To three generations of midwestern motorists, the Red Crown meant gasoline.

and tractor use among America's farmers, and Standard began emphasizing sales of Red Crown gasoline and Polarine lubricants at company-owned and operated stations affiliated with its bulk plants. Red Crown and Polarine were the first branded petroleum products to achieve name recognition in the Midwest.

Unfortunately, though, Standard faced much the same dilemma that Jersey and Socony did, in that refiner-marketers were separated from their crude supply sources in the

This early Standard station served motorists in Robinson, Kansas, in about 1924. ***Patrick Shimmin***

breakup of Standard Oil. In the earliest years, Standard was heavily dependent on one of its former Standard siblings, Prairie Oil and Gas, for crude supplies. Standard's first venture into production came in 1919, when Standard purchased control of Dixie Oil Company whose production centered in the newly developed Louisiana fields. In 1920, Standard purchased a minority interest in Wyoming-based Midwest Oil Company. At the time of the purchase, Midwest was involved in developing production from oil fields in the Rocky Mountain area and had sufficient excess production to supply crude oil for Standard's refining and marketing needs.

In 1922, Standard was the first company to market a premium grade gasoline. Branded Solite, it was a marginally successful product but garnered enough of a customer base to remain on the market after Standard secured an agreement to market GM's Ethyl gasoline after the initial experimentation involving Refiners Oil Company. Standard stations in Richmond, Indiana, began marketing Red Crown Ethyl in March 1924, and later that year, Standard obtained an exclusive agreement to market Ethyl throughout its territory. An opportunity to team up with GM to produce tetraethyl lead was tabled. Meanwhile, Jersey stepped in to create the Ethyl Gasoline Corporation in conjunction with General Motors in August 1924, leaving Standard simply as a licensee. The missed opportunity turned out to be a blessing in disguise. In March 1925, tragedy struck. Several employees of the Ethyl research and manufacturing facilities in New Jersey died from exposure to the chemical. Sales of Ethylized gasoline were suspended by the U.S. Surgeon General until studies could be made of the long-term effects of exposure to the product. After more than a year of health-related studies, Ethyl was reintroduced to the markets on the condition that it be premixed at the terminals as opposed to the common practice of metering tetraethyl lead into gasoline directly at the retail pumps.

Standard's "regular" grade gasoline was identified by Red Crown.

Red Crown Ethyl identified the "premium" grade.

Standard's exclusive agreement was discarded by the new company, but it did retain the rights to distribute Ethylized gasoline under the Red Crown Ethyl brand.

In 1926, Standard adopted the earliest version of its famed torch logo. Until that time, Standard was identified entirely by the Red Crown, emblem of its most famous product. Although well recognized, the Red Crown was insufficient for corporatewide recognition since it represented only gasoline. A search for a new emblem to represent the corporation focused on the traditions of the corporation. Chosen was a flaming torch, symbolizing the company's original business, kerosene for illumination. The torch was superimposed over the word "Service" on a blue field. Although Red Crown and the other various color crowns would continue to represent Standard's gasolines, the new logo was applied to station structures, packaged products, and some signage. Despite the adoption of the corporate logo, station signage remained plain, simply "Standard Service" in white on a blue field until the torch and oval logo was created in 1945.

In 1916, just as Standard began searching for outside sources of crude oil, an international oil exploration and trading company was being assembled from various holdings to form Pan American Trading and Transport Company. Pan-Am was born big, much like Sinclair Oil Company which had formed that same year. Within a year or two Pan-Am had expanded from its core business of foreign and domestic oil production and was involved in Gulf Coast refining. A production division that operated in California as well had been very successful and was marketing under the Pan-Gas brand in

The "sub-regular" grade, Solite (later Blue Crown).

This Standard "Stanolind Aviation" globe displays the early corporate logo.

California. In the early 1920s, Pan-Am formed Mexican Petroleum Company, named for its primary source of crude oil. Mexican began gasoline marketing in New York and New England under the Pan-Am brand name. In 1923, Pan-Am purchased a 50 percent interest in a small Baltimore refining and marketing company that would prove to be the most important investment Pan-Am would ever make.

Baltimore-based American Oil Company had been formed in 1910 to refine kerosene for retail distribution as heating oil in Baltimore. In 1915, American developed a superior gasoline-benzol blend and began marketing this unique motor fuel under the trademark Amoco-Gas at a chain of service stations in Baltimore. Amoco-Gas met with immediate acceptance by Baltimore motorists who had wearied of lower quality fuels and the damage caused by them. By 1920, Amoco-Gas was available throughout Maryland, in Washington D.C., and in the Virginia suburbs, and expansion was limited only by the availability of crude oil. Into the picture came crude-rich Pan-Am. In 1923, the Blaustein family, owners of American Oil, traded a 50 percent interest in their company to Pan-American in exchange for a guaranteed ten-year crude oil supply contract. At the end of ten years, Pan American would have the option of purchasing the remaining portion of American Oil.

Shortly after Pan-Am purchased interest in American, a group of investors purchased an interest in Pan-Am. The investors brought in Standard for financial backing and experience. Seeing the value of Pan-Am's crude oil reserves and transportation network, Standard purchased a large interest in Pan American in 1925. Almost forgotten in the merger was Pan American's investment in the small Baltimore refining and marketing firm, American Oil.

With Standard's purchase of Pan-American, formerly all-domestic Standard became an international oil company overnight and gained the marketing outlets of the Mexican Petroleum Company in New England and the newly formed network of bulk plants and service stations bearing the Pan-Am brand across the South. Also, Standard inherited Pan-Am's 50 percent interest in American Oil and its rapidly expanding chain of Lord Baltimore Filling Stations, which sold Amoco-Gas in the mid-Atlantic area. Pan American Eastern Petroleum Corporation was created as a Standard subsidiary to operate the Pan-Am refining and marketing functions. Barely three years later, Standard purchased the remaining portions of Midwest Oil Company to gain virtually complete self-sufficiency in crude oil production. Along with Midwest's production and refining, Standard gained retail marketing that Midwest had assembled over the previous several years in Wyoming, Colorado, and Montana and Midwest's subsidiary, Utah Oil Refining Company, with marketing facilities in Utah and Idaho. The former Midwest stations were branded Standard, as the brand had been assigned to Continental Oil in those areas and was not in use. The Utah Oil Refining stations were branded Vico/Pep, brand names acquired from previous mergers.

At the onset of the Depression, the decision was made to sell Pan American's foreign operations, which consisted of production, refining, and marketing properties all over the world. There were several reasons for the move, not the least of which was the desire to concentrate all efforts into domestic production, which was less susceptible to governmental actions. Jersey opted to purchase the overseas operations in a complex deal that included a guaranteed supply of refined products for sale by Pan American's affiliate, American. Many of these properties would have been lost to expropriation or war over the next fifteen years, indicating Standard's incredible foresight into world oil policy and events that would shape it.

Standard's Pan American Petroleum purchased the balance of American Oil Company in 1933, and American's Amoco brand replaced the Pan-Am brand at stations in New York and New England. Mexican petroleum was dissolved, and assets were assigned to American Oil as well. Pan-Am stations in Georgia and Florida rebranded Amoco as well, and the famed Amoco-Gas, known since 1932 simply as Amoco, was a market leader from Maine to Florida. American Oil's founders, the Blaustein family, gained a substantial interest in Standard as a result of the merger and would remain influential in the corporation for many years to follow. With this realignment of brands, Standard and its affiliates would continue to market throughout most of the United

Glass, and later plastic flames, topped the Standard, Pan-Am, and Utoco major signs introduced in 1946 and used until 1961. Despite rumors, these never appeared on gas pumps, except perhaps when placed there by some enterprising dealer.

Amoco's Baltimore station was typical of those constructed by all the major oil companies in the 1920s and early 1930s. This one still stands outside Newport News, Virginia.

States under four different brands: Standard, Pan-Am, Amoco, and Vico/Pep 88 (later Utoco) until 1961.

right
Amoco, Standard, Pan-Am, and Utoco collectibles are publicly displayed at Stancil Oil Company's Amoco Museum in Selma, North Carolina. Shown here is owner Larry Stancil with a part of the display.

To secure equipment for company, jobber, and dealer use at advantageous prices, Standard entered into an agreement with two of the Standard siblings, Socony-Vacuum and Conoco, as well as Sun Oil, to purchase gasoline pump manufacturer Martin and Schwartz. From 1937 until 1949, the four companies controlled the pump manufacturer, and stations displaying the brands of these companies were able to buy equipment direct from the manufacturer and save significantly over competing marketers. The arrangement was identical to the advantage Jersey had long enjoyed with its ownership of Gilbert and Barker Manufacturing of Springfield, Massachusetts. Gilbert and Barker had originally been a unit of the Standard Oil

Amoco products were offered as part of the product mix at Hop's Place garage and auto parts store in Hampton, Virginia, in 1938.

AMERICAN
AMOCO
GAS
AMOCO
AMOCO
AMOCO
AMOCO

This unusual "middle of the block" Pan-Am station was operating on Memphis' Chelsea Avenue in 1939. ***Chip Flohe***

Trust but was assigned to Jersey with the 1911 breakup. Jersey would remain in control for most of the rest of this century, giving Jersey-branded operators a distinct buying advantage.

Another piece of the Standard puzzle was added in 1939 when Standard purchased Standard Oil Company of Nebraska. Standard of Nebraska had been organized in 1906 to circumvent Nebraska laws that barred Standard of Indiana from operating there. It was essentially a marketing operation and was almost totally dependent upon Standard of Indiana for its products. Standard of Nebraska remained a separate subsidiary until 1944, and the bar and circle logo used by Standard of Nebraska remained in place until the new torch and oval was phased in at all Standard locations after World War II. The Standard brand and all rights to other Standard trademarks, Red Crown, Polarine, and so forth, were now controlled by Standard of Indiana in a fourteen-state area of America's heartland.

Wartime gave Standard many reasons to be thankful that it had divested itself of most foreign holdings early on. As a result, Standard fared better than most other companies during

A not-so-typical Pan-Am station from the postwar era, Knoxville, Tennessee. ***Chip Flohe***

An economy grade Pan-Am pump globe from the 1930s.

World War II. Immediately following the war, Standard mounted a reimaging like none other in its history. The Standard Torch, in use for nearly twenty years in the corporate logo, was added to a new tri-color oval to create an entirely new corporate and marketing logo that would be used, with one minor revision and two major revisions, until the present day. In order to unify the various brands, the new logo appeared in three versions, with "Standard" on the center

A postwar Pan-Am minor sign with porcelain flame instead of illuminated glass.

band for use in the Midwest, "Pan-Am" in the South, and "Utoco" in the far West. The new brand, Utoco, an acronym for Utah Oil Refining Company, replaced the dated "Vico/Pep 88" brand. The Amoco stations in the East, still partially under the control of the Blaustein family through their ownership of Pan-American and Standard stock, retained their famed red-and-black oval Amoco emblem. The new Pan-Am logo was seen in two new states following the war as well, with the addition of marketing in Arkansas and Kentucky. The early 1950s saw the introduction of the Amoco brand, and oddly enough, the eastern Amoco oval logo, into several select Texas markets, filling in several very noticeable gaps in Standard's marketing territory. Coast-to-coast marketing was not so very far into the future, and Standard remained a marketing leader.

When Pan-American Eastern Petroleum gained control of American Oil in 1933, the Blaustein family, founders of Pan-Am affiliate American Oil, acquired a substantial portion of the minority stock in Pan-American. In essence, the Blausteins became joint owners of Pan-American along with Standard and others. This arrangement gave the Blausteins seats on the Pan-Am board of directors, where they faced off against Standard-interest directors on a number of major issues. Litigation continued through the

This early flanged sign identified locations where Standard of Nebraska products could be bought. ***Mike Douglass***

1940s, and the unresolved differences between the companies contributed to the fact that the Amoco brand was exempted from the general marketing reimaging that Standard and the other brands participated in 1945. After nearly twenty years of disagreement and lawsuits, the Blaustein family agreed to an exchange of Pan-American stock for Standard stock in 1954. American and Pan-Am were completely absorbed by Standard, and plans were made to replace the Pan-Am brand in its six-state territory with Amoco's brand and famous unleaded benzol premium grade motor fuel. Pan-Am stations received signage indicating they were "Distributors of Amoco Products." In 1956, Pan-Am signs were replaced with a new torch and oval, emblazoned with the name Amoco. Stations in the traditional eastern American Oil territory retained their red-and-black oval logo, but product containers sold through these outlets could display either or both of the logos.

As other Standard affiliates expanded coast-to-coast, Standard sought out a way to enter the West Coast markets. In 1960, Standard's Utah Oil Refining division purchased Spokane, Washington-based True's Oil Company. True's had marketed under the Rainbow brand in the Pacific Northwest for more than thirty years at the time. Rainbow stations became Utoco stations overnight, and Standard had its Pacific Coast entry into more lucrative California markets.

In December 1960, Standard announced a major realignment of domestic marketing. While the corporate name would remain Standard Oil

Standard marketed Polarine oils from before the 1911 breakup until 1961. *Jack Heiman*

This sign identified one of the many Standard filling stations across the Midwest. *Jack Heiman*

Assorted Standard signs from the 1920s, now in a private collection. ***Jack Heiman***

Company of Indiana, all domestic marketing was assigned to a subsidiary they named American Oil Company. Standard stations in fourteen midwestern states would remain branded Standard, but those Amoco stations in the East and South and Utoco stations in the far West were branded American. A revised torch and oval logo was introduced to herald the rebranding and reimaging, titled in corporate advertising as "The Big Step," commemorating American's big step across the country from East Coast to West Coast markets. In the early 1960s, the American brand was expanded into California, Nevada, New Mexico, and Arizona as well, although these areas remained marginal marketing areas for American. The brand would not survive the 1970s shortages in markets on the West Coast.

For more than fifty years after Standard Oil was broken up and Standard affiliates were assigned the various trademarks of the company for use in their respective territories, two of the trademarks, Red Crown gasoline and Polarine motor oil, remained in use by Standard of Indiana. Long after other affiliates had abandoned the venerable trademarks, Standard proudly displayed its beautiful Red Crown globes atop gas pumps across the Midwest. Other colors had graced the globes, White Crown, Blue Crown, Gold Crown, and others, but Red Crown meant Standard to many motorists. The tradition ended with the 1961 reimaging, though, as gasolines sold at Standard outlets were renamed American Regular and American Premium, replacing Red Crown (regular) and

LOW COST
PER MILE
RED
CROWN

Gold Crown (premium). In the East, Amoco-Gas, and later just Amoco, had identified an unusual gasoline-benzol blend that did not depend on tetraethyl lead to increase antiknock properties. Capitalizing on this unusual fuel, the gasoline was renamed Amoco Super Premium, and decals on pumps advertised it as "The Only One, Certified Lead Free." It continued to be a market leader, as it does to this day. Motor oil brand names were realigned as well, and Polarine disappeared from product lists, while Permalube and Super Permalube cans, along with others that would be offered through either American or Standard stations, displayed a "no-name" torch and oval that appeared anywhere advertising could not be brand specific.

This torch and oval logo, carrying the American and Standard brand names or simply a torch with no name, was revised again in 1971. Motor oils and other packaged products that could be sold at stations using either sign received a brand name from history, Amoco. American Oil Company became Amoco Oil Company in 1973, and in 1974 American stations rebranded Amoco, while the Amoco name was added to stations in Standard territory. Station signage remains Standard in many areas today, but the company and its gasolines are now known nationwide as Amoco. As unleaded fuels were mandated in the 1970s, Amoco's sixty years of experience in manufacturing unleaded fuels gave Amoco products a reputation for top quality in the marketplace.

During the 1980s, Amoco quickly embraced the convenience store concept, creating the prototype Amoco Food Shop design for use by Amoco jobbers nationwide. Amoco remained loyal to dealers and automotive service in many markets as well, with automotive services advertised and warranted by Amoco CertiCare Centers. Today, in the 1990s, with nearly 10,000 stations in the thirty states that had been the core territory for Standard, Amoco, and Pan-Am, Amoco Corporation, as Standard Oil of Indiana is now known, enjoys a customer preference advantage that other marketers could only dream about. Amoco was called "The Original Special Motor Fuel" in the 1930s, and Amoco Ultimate, as the product is known today, remains the brand perceived to be highest in quality among all gasoline available today.

Rare Utoco and Standard Marine fuel globes. ***Peter Capell***

left
An unusual die-cut Red Crown sign from the 1920s. ***Jack Heiman***

Standard Oil Company of California–Chevron Corporation

Standard of California, or Socal as it will be known in this chapter, was a relatively recent creation of Standard Oil at the time of the breakup. In 1900, Standard purchased the Pacific Coast Oil Company, founded in 1879 as the first major producer of California crude. Also in 1879, Standard had opened a sales office in California, and with the dissolution of the trust in 1892 and the subsequent creation of Standard Oil Company of New Jersey, marketing in California and other parts of the West had been assigned to Standard Oil Company of Iowa. Pacific Coast was a major force in California production at the time it was absorbed by Standard, and in 1906 Pacific Coast's production, refining, and transportation capabilities were combined with Standard Oil of Iowa's marketing abilities to create Standard Oil Company of California.

Socal's first attribute was to develop what we consider to be the first retail filling station in America. In 1907, the bulk plant operator in Seattle, Washington, had wearied of automobile owners interrupting the routine functions of his plant. At curbside he installed an old water-heater tank on a stand, piped it to a bulk gasoline storage tank, and attached a shutoff valve and garden hose. Seattle motorists could simply pull up alongside the bulk plant fence, insert the hose into the car's tank,

This 1941 map displays the classic Standard logo with Socal's version of the red crown. It includes an early version of the modern Chevron logo.

STANDARD OIL PRODUCTS

in

ALABAMA
FLORIDA
GEORGIA
KENTUCKY
MISSISSIPPI

include among many others

CROWN GASOLINE
CROWN EXTRA GASOLINE
ESSO MOTOR OILS
MOBILOIL MOTOR OIL
ATLAS TIRES & TUBES
ATLAS BATTERIES
AUTO ACCESSORIES

AT YOUR STANDARD OIL DEALER

HELMLY'S SERVICE STATION 115-14
37th & OGEECHEE ROAD
Phone 9794 - Savannah, Ga.

AND AT STANDARD OIL DEALERS ALL ALONG THE WAY

EASTERN UNITED STATES

Interstate Travel Guide

STANDARD OIL COMPANY
INCORPORATED IN KENTUCKY

In 1946, Standard Oil Company of Kentucky, commonly called Kyso, was marketing Esso and Mobil motor oils in addition to Crown and Crown Extra gasolines, supplied by Esso.

open the valve, and gravity fill did the rest. The filling station was born. Unimaginable in that day was the time, not so far into the future, when stations dispensing Socal gasoline would become the most common commercial sight in the western United States.

With the breakup of Standard Oil in 1911, Socal emerged as perhaps the most integrated of the newly independent companies. Left with California production, refinery capacity, transportation facilities, and bulk marketing facilities throughout California, Oregon, Washington,

Standard of California's "red crown."

Idaho, Nevada, Utah, and Arizona, Socal was functionally independent. In 1915, Socal launched a filling station construction program and began promoting the Standard Red Crown gasoline to western motorists. In this era, Socal developed Zerolene, a premium motor oil noted for temperature stability in the extremely cold climates of the northern portions of the territory.

Without the need to purchase independent companies to secure much needed crude, Socal did nothing to expand its marketing territory in the early years, content to blanket the western United States with company-owned stations dispensing Red Crown gasoline and Zerolene oil. Only in the late 1920s did Socal look toward expansion. About 1926, the company established an office in El Paso to oversee oil exploration in Texas. Texas had long forbidden any Standard company from operating within its borders and at about that time had opened the door to Standard exploration. Jersey had, in fact, been in Texas for more than five years at that time, but only through the secret ownership of controlling interest in Humble. Socal chose the name Pasotex Petroleum for its Texas operation, and several years later when laws limiting Standard's influence in Texas were repealed, Pasotex became the Standard Oil Company of Texas. Pasotex's original purpose was exploration, but by 1930 the company was marketing Red Crown gasoline and Zerolene oils through a

The Chevron brand was introduced in 1945 to unify the products sold by the various Standard of California divisions.

dealer network in Texas and New Mexico. Standard Oil Company of British Columbia had also been formed, and Standard gasolines were marketed in that province as well.

To ease the long-term effects of the Depression, Socal decided to concentrate on lubricants, a higher profit business than gasoline. In 1935, Socal developed a superior motor oil it named RPM and almost immediately began soliciting lubricants jobbers in select markets nationwide. Also in about 1935, Socal decided to expand its retail gasoline marketing into the

Calso was the marketing name selected for Socal's Rocky Mountain marketing expansion.

left
Flight was Socal's economy "motor" grade gasoline in the 1930s. The "green arrow" version was used at Calso-branded stations.

below
Shown here are assorted Socal collectibles, displayed today in a private collection.

growing Rocky Mountain region. With restrictions on the use of the Standard name, Socal established a subsidiary, the California Company, to operate bulk plants and solicit dealers, branded Calso, throughout the Rocky Mountain and western plains region, in Colorado, Wyoming, Montana, North and South Dakota, and Nebraska. Experience with independent dealers in the Rockies and in Texas prompted Socal to build its dealer network in California as well. Company-operated stations were assigned to a new subsidiary, Standard Stations, Inc., while the dealer network was

This 1930s dealer station was typical of those throughout the West. ***Ron Johnson***

branded simply as Standard Oil Dealers. Dealer stations in the Rockies offered products similar to those sold on the West Coast, but they were offered under a green-white-and-blue color scheme that contrasted greatly with Standard's traditional red-white-and-blue outlets elsewhere.

During the 1930s, Socal had become an international oil company with the discovery of vast amounts of crude in Saudi Arabia. So much crude was available that Socal had formed a partnership with Texaco to tie Socal's production to Texaco's refining and marketing structure in the eastern hemisphere. Texaco stations throughout Africa and Asia were rebranded Caltex, the trademark chosen by the new joint venture operation named Arabian American Oil Company. With this move, Socal had grown beyond adolescence to adulthood.

World War II interrupted Socal's ever-expanding scope, and much of the war saw Socal people safeguarding Arabian oil fields. At home, gasoline rationing diminished retail profits, while Socal had become an innovator by hiring women to replace men as service station attendants during the war. At the close of World War II, Socal again expanded its retail presence, this time to the heart of Jersey marketing territory. In 1945, Standard purchased Monogram Manufacturing Company of Perth Amboy, New Jersey. Monogram was a lubricants manufacturer with terminal facilities in the metropolitan New York area. Socal recruited a dealer network to be supplied from these terminals and established the Calso brand in major cities from Maine to Virginia.

The "Chevron Gas Station" image replaced the Calso name in the Rockies after World War II. ***Patrick Shimmin***

Socal had used a tri-band "hallmark" chevron logo before World War II, in conjunction with the Standard Stations, Inc., brand name. At the close of the war, gasolines sold at Standard or Calso stations were changed from Standard gasoline and Standard Ethyl to Chevron and Chevron Supreme in the Rocky Mountain areas and along the West Coast. Capitalizing on the name recognition but using a logo that did not include the hallmark design, Calso stations and Standard Oil dealer stations became Chevron Gas Stations with a cream-maroon-and-green color scheme. Pumps, minor signage, and globes retained the traditional red, white, and blue, as did the company operated Standard Stations, Inc., along the West Coast. Calso stations in the East, still relatively few in number, were not affected by this change. The hallmark logo was incorporated into the RPM "rotation" logo as well, increasing its recognition in those parts of the country where only Socal's lubricants were sold. Also of note is that by this time, stations under the hallmark had been added in Alaska and Hawaii as well.

The Chevron brand had been introduced in the East by the time this 1968 photo was taken in Oak Ridge, Tennessee. ***Chip Flohe***

Never content to maintain the status quo, in 1957 the hallmark logo was added to a shield-shaped trademark that appeared in

This pump sign was used in Calso markets in the Northeast in the 1950s. ***Mark McKeown Collection***

maroon with "Chevron Dealer" in the upper field, or in blue with "Standard Station" in the upper field. Two years later, in an unprecedented thirty-day reimaging, Calso stations from Maine to Virginia adopted the logo, with "Chevron Station (or Dealer)" appearing on an upper blue field. Chevron gasoline was now available coast-to-coast.

Socal's next marketing expansion ranks as probably the all-time coup in petroleum marketing. In 1961, Standard Oil Company of Kentucky, commonly called Kyso, was purchased outright by

This sign identified Chevron-branded stations operated by Socal affiliate Standard Oil of Texas. ***Mike Douglass Collection***

Socal. Kyso was addressed in the chapter on Jersey, as Kyso had served as a giant jobber for Jersey products for essentially all of its fifty-year independent history. Although no Esso signs appeared in Kentucky, Georgia, Florida, Alabama, or Mississippi, the Esso trademark was well known in those Kyso states since Kyso had long marketed Esso motor oils and other lubricants. It, too, was hardly a secret that Kyso's Crown and Crown Extra were actually Esso and Esso Extra gasolines under a different brand. With the purchase of Kyso by Socal, all Jersey supply contracts were phased out as rapidly as possible. Kyso stations were reimaged, and gasolines were renamed Chevron and Chevron Supreme to conform with products sold in other parts of the country.

Long involved in direct retailing of gasoline through company-owned stations, Socal began an immediate expansion program by building company-owned and operated Kyso Standard Oil stations at an ever-increasing number of interstate interchanges. Kyso quickly progressed from the image of a small town, jobber-oriented marketer to that of a major oil company. So successful was the interstate expansion that stations were constructed in adjacent states. With restrictions on the use of the Standard Oil brand in Tennessee, Virginia, and South Carolina, the Chevron logo was proudly displayed on these Standard Oil look—alike locations, ever more tying together the Kyso Standard Oil and Chevron images. With this market expansion, Chevron gasoline could be found in all states from Maine to Florida and west to the Mississippi, and from Texas north through the Great Plains and west to the Pacific Coast.

An interesting sideline of Socal marketing came to an end in 1967 when Jersey purchased the Signal stations along the West Coast and rebranded them Enco. Signal Oil Company began building a network of gasoline stations in California in 1932, but in 1947 sold the entire marketing operation, along with the famed Signal brand, to Socal. Socal operated the Signal dealer network as a secondary brand for some twenty years in much the same way that Sinclair operated the Richfield of New York operations for more than thirty years. Although Signal re-entered gasoline marketing in 1950 with the purchase

This Standard Oil of Kentucky pump globe was in use prior to 1920.

Hernando, Mississippi, was home to this 1962 Standard Oil station. ***Chip Flohe***

of Bankline Oil Company, those stations owned or supplied by Signal bore Bankline's Norwalk brand. Later mergers brought such diverse brands as Hancock and Billups into the Signal family, but Signal would never again market under its own name.

In 1970, the Chevron and Standard images were reworked, with stations receiving a new design and color scheme. The hallmark logo was reworked, with a modern, more rounded appearance. Standard Oil stations in the Southeast became simply "Standard" stations with this reimaging. The Chevron brand was added to motor oil and lubricants containers sold by all Chevron, Standard, and Standard Oil stations. Prior to this, the hallmark logo or the logo with the RPM rotation appeared on cans, with no reference to either Standard or Chevron. Slowly a way was being made to eliminate the Standard name, with its regional restrictions, and present a unified marketing presence all across America. In 1977, the "Standard" brand was removed from station signage in all but a few token outlets, kept in place at only one or two stations in each state to avoid forfeiting the rights to the famed trademark.

In 1984, Socal, now Chevron Corporation, was a partner in the largest merger in the oil industry until that time. In 1984, Chevron merged with an ailing, Pittsburgh-based Gulf Oil, essentially rescuing the company from a hostile takeover bid by corporate raider T. Boone Pickens and others. With the merger, Chevron added Gulf's exploration, transportation, and refining capabilities to its own and converted Gulf stations in states where Chevron had little representation to Chevron. Virginia, West

A typical Standard of Kentucky flange sign from about 1920.

A postwar neon Standard Oil (Kyso) sign, displayed here in a private collection. *Bruce Miller*

In 1970, Standard began rebranding all of its stations to Chevron. This station in Florida in 1970 displays both brand names. *Walt Wimer, Jr.*

Standard motor oils were sold nationwide under the "RPM" trademark beginning in 1935. Shown here are assorted cans from those years.

Virginia, Maryland, and Delaware saw a huge increase in the number of Chevron outlets, and some stations were added in Texas, Oklahoma, Louisiana, and Arkansas as well. Those Gulf stations in the Southeast, where Chevron was already well represented from the Kyso merger, were sold to BP America, and those in the Northeast, former Calso territory, were sold off to an independent convenience store operator, Cumberland Farms, which continues to use the Gulf brand today. On the heels of the merger, Chevron began streamlining its operation, abandoning the Northeast and some areas of the Great Plains as well.

By 1990, Chevron had wholeheartedly embraced the convenience store concept, with many West Coast company-owned outlets and thousands of jobber outlets coast-to-coast being rebuilt as convenience stores. Marketing focused on a gasoline performance additive, Techroline, blended with Chevron gasolines and being sold as an aftermarket additive, giving Chevron gasoline the perception of being among the highest quality in the marketplace. As of Standard's 125th anniversary in 1995, Chevron, with assets in excess of $34 billion, marketed through nearly 8,000 stations in twenty-seven states.

This 1930s Crown globe is the only Kyso globe that displays the company name.

Standard Oil Company of Ohio–BP America

The original. Standard Oil Company (Ohio), as it emerged from the breakup, was the much pared-down remnant of Rockefeller's original creation. It seems the court took particular vengeance on Standard Oil of Ohio, which will be called Sohio in our text. Sohio was left with only the Cleveland refinery and marketing throughout Ohio. Making the most of what it had, Sohio concentrated on becoming a market leader. Sohio was among the first to consider retail gasoline marketing a viable business function for a refiner-marketer. The company's bulk plants and sales offices throughout Ohio gave it the basis for the most retail-minded business philosophy of any of the Standard companies.

Globe-topped pumps identify Sohio products on this 1934 road map of Ohio (where else?).

Sohio was assigned the Standard, Red Crown, and Polarine brand names for use in Ohio only. It was operating a drive-through fueling facility at a Columbus bulk plant within a year of the breakup and by 1916 had pioneered a standardized station design, known as Type A, suitable for all types of locations, from which Red Crown gasoline and Polarine oil could be dispensed. Sohio was content to buy crude from outside sources in the early years and had sufficient marketing to support the construction of a new refinery in Toledo in the early 1920s. Crude oil developments actually harmed Sohio's profitability. Rich in domestic crude and with excess refining capacity, midwestern marketers such as Sinclair entered Ohio markets to wrest away some of Sohio's 80 percent-plus share of the state's gasoline market, knowing full well that being "brand-locked" as a one-state marketer, Sohio had no means of retaliation in its core markets and no auxiliary markets to fall back

This elaborate crown identified Standard of Ohio's Red Crown gasoline to Ohio motorists.

on. As other marketers discovered Sohio's dilemma, the Ohio market, with its industrial base and relatively high numbers of motorists, attracted many new entrants to gasoline marketing.

To counteract the effects of increasing competition, Sohio elected to turn its sales force into a highly trained and highly motivated retail marketing organization, making filling stations operate much like chain stores such as A&P. A new image was developed, as red-white-and-blue had been adopted by many other Standard affiliates and had come to represent Standard gasoline nationwide, as did the marketing brand name Sohio, taken from the corporate name "The Standard Oil Company (Ohio)." Station personnel received a vigorous indoctrination with company marketing philosophy, and Sohio stations became very profitable retail stores for purchasing automotive fuels and oils. Sohio was among the first to add service bays to most of its stations and actively participated in the cooperative formed in 1930 by various Standard affiliates and Atlas Corporation to market automotive items, known in the trade as TBA, for Tires, Batteries, and Accessories. Backed by a nationwide guarantee with warranty service available through virtually all of the stations that had repair facilities that bore the various brands of Standard of Ohio, New Jersey, California, Indiana, and Kentucky, Atlas gave these companies a TBA line they could call their own and made the term "filling station" obsolete, allowing filling stations to truly become "service stations."

Sohio, too, was among the first marketers to develop a "super-station" concept. Thwarted only by excessive cost and low returns during the Depression, the fabulous Sohio "English

In Ohio, it simply meant gasoline. ***Mike Douglass Collection***

These porcelain banners were used as secondary signs at Sohio stations in the early 1930s. ***Mike Douglass Collection***

Lodge" stations expanded on Pure's successful cottage design then in use by adding service areas and customer lounges like those found in upscale department stores. A number of these units were built, but cost restrictions of the Depression era prevented this new marketing concept to fully take shape.

Although Sohio could not use its valued Standard-related trademarks outside Ohio, nothing prevented the company from entering other markets under other brand names. Sohio chose the route of purchasing existing marketing operations, the first of which was Wheeling, West Virginia-based Spears and Riddle. Spears and Riddle was a wholesale marketer, essentially a terminal company, that distributed gasoline from New York to the Gulf Coast. Independent

This pump globe from the late 1920s identified Sohio's "premium" Ethyl gasoline.

marketers purchasing from Spears and Riddle were offered use of the brand name Fleet-Wing. When Sohio completed the purchase, it established the Fleet-Wing Corporation, based in Cleveland, Ohio, as a brand for independent jobbers in Pennsylvania, West Virginia, Michigan, and Ohio in limited numbers. This split operation—corporate Sohio stations and jobber Fleet-Wing stations—served to foster the image of two separate companies to those motorists who pre-

This rare outboard fuel globe was the only Sohio globe ever to display the full Sohio logo.

ferred not to do business with a Standard company. Moreover, it made Sohio less dependent on Ohio markets and gave it a brand to retaliate with out-of-state marketers.

Next came Refiners Oil Company, the Dayton, Ohio-based markets in southern Ohio and southeastern Indiana. Refiners had been the original distributor of Ethyl gasoline, when Dayton-based General Motors Research Labs needed a company through which to test market its tetraethyl lead additive. Although Indiana Standard and Jersey Standard would come to dominate the Ethyl operation, Jersey being a partner in the creation of Ethyl Gasoline Corporation, it was tiny Refiners Oil that had led the way. Refiners' more than 250 stations were rebranded Sohio in 1930.

During the 1930s, Sohio sought out ways to offset the effects of the Depression by shifting profit centers to those areas not so dependent upon the ordinary consumer. Sohio purchased a Standard sibling, Solar Refining, increasing its refining capacity and solidifying its refining position. Sohio began developing a pipeline network, both for crude oil gathering and product distribution, minimizing the company's transportation costs and allowing it to make spot market purchases of crude when pricing advantages arose.

Recovery was successful, and nearly complete, when World War II erupted. Sohio, as a manufacturer of sorts, joined the wartime effort to manufacture badly needed aviation fuels and lubricants and was a leading supplier of these fuels to the armed services. Crude exploration and production was intensified as well, in support of the refineries and their efforts. When the war ended, Sohio returned to its position as Ohio's dominant gasoline marketer, and postwar expansion and service station development was intensified. Sohio stations of the area sported a distinctive art moderne look, and differed from competing stations with an open-air design that did not partition off automotive service areas from sales offices and showrooms.

In another marketing expansion move, Sohio purchased Canfield, Ohio-based Canfield Oil Company. Founded in 1886, Canfield originally had been a lubricants manufacturer. Its Wm. Penn motor oils were among the first branded oils to be distributed over a large region of the country and were highly regarded as one

Boron and Extron were brand names for Sohio gasoline in the 1950s. Extron, the regular grade, was offered in a marine fuel as well.

of the top-quality motor oils in the early automotive era. At the time of the Sohio purchase, Canfield branded more than 200 stations in Ohio and Pennsylvania. Sohio operated Canfield stations, later Wm. Penn stations, as a secondary brand until the 1980s. In the early 1960s, an effort was made to establish the Wm. Penn brand of motor oils as an automotive jobber brand; that is, one that was sold primarily through auto parts distributors. The plan was never widely accepted, although Wm. Penn oils were marketed until after the BP brand replaced Sohio brands in 1990.

In the early 1950s, Sohio was among the first of the major oil companies to look beyond lubricants into other petrochemical products, particularly those for agricultural use. Existing sales channels were available, and Sohio chemical products became well known throughout the state. Sohio was also the first marketer to discover that by adding the chemical element boron to gasoline, antiknock performance was improved and engine wear was reduced. In 1954, Sohio introduced Sohio Boron Supreme, replacing Sohio Supreme as its premium grade product. Two years later, Sohio decided to enter markets outside Ohio with company-owned, retail-oriented stations in areas where its affiliate brands, Fleet-Wing and Canfield, had been successful. To avoid directly identifying its jobber brands with Sohio, company stations outside Ohio displayed the brand name Boron on station signage. Boron Oil became a Sohio subsidiary, and the first Boron signs were installed at stations in the Kentucky suburbs of Cincinnati, where Sohio operated a refinery. The brand was expanded several years later, as Boron stations appeared in West Virginia and Pennsylvania, particularly the Pittsburgh area. These would become strongholds for the Boron brand in years to follow.

When the brand name Sohio was introduced in 1928, station signage consisted of an oval with a diamond-like design forming triangles over the word "Sohio" on a center band. The logo saw several revisions but by 1960 was looking somewhat dated. In addition, the signs did not reproduce well for use in the large signage needed at interstate off-ramps. In 1962, Sohio introduced a new logo, an oval shield with an inner oval bearing either the Sohio or Boron brand names. Stations were reimaged as well, and many received a new design with side entry bays, hiding automotive work from direct roadside view, allowing for more decorative landscaping then being mandated by many metropolitan zoning boards. The new logo was incorporated into station design as well and was proudly displayed on structural walls.

Canfield Oil Company was another of the Ohio marketing firms absorbed by Sohio.

The Boron brand grew rapidly in the early 1960s, and by 1968, Boron entered Michigan markets and was being added to a number of truck stop facilities and other unconventional service stations of the era. Tie-ins with food service and lodging operations, although not unusual in the 1960s, seemed to indicate something of the look of today's convenience store/fast food combination units. Sohio's retail orientation and chain of company-operated stations gave them opportunity to experiment with various marketing concepts, some of which led to today's service station designs. To ensure a consistent image, the company opted to concentrate primarily on company-owned and

Wheeling, West Virginia-based Spears and Riddle introduced the Fleet Wing brand. Sohio purchased the company in the late 1920s but continued to use the Fleet Wing trademark as a secondary brand until 1968.

operated or company-owned, dealer-leased stations. Sohio sold off the Fleet-Wing operation to Pennzoil in 1968. Fleet-Wing stations in Ohio, West Virginia, and Pennsylvania were eventually converted to the Pennzoil brand, virtually all of them prior to 1980.

In spite of its success in the retail marketplace, Sohio suffered from lack of crude oil production. By the 1960s, Sohio was involved in some domestic production, alone or in combination with other companies. Its crude-gathering pipeline network led from all major production fields to its refineries. Still Sohio was little more than a regional oil company, ranking below such regional entities as Pure, Union, and DX in assets, sales, and profits. Sohio management saw the wisdom in growth and self-sufficiency, and in the growth-through-merger days of the 1960s, Sohio began to look for a crude-rich partner with which to team up.

British Petroleum was founded as an exploration company in the early years of this

The Standard C
SOHIO GASOLINE

Neon signage illuminates this suburban Sohio station in about 1954. ***Joe and Judy Gross***

left
In the late 1920s, Sohio introduced this English Tudor station design. Few of these stations were built before the Depression, which made them economically unfeasible. ***Joe and Judy Gross***

century and was owned in part by the British government. Very successful and profitable, British Petroleum, commonly called BP, was a world leader in petroleum by the time it entered North American markets in the late 1950s with a small number of stations in Canada. In the late 1960s, BP exploration tenacity paid off, and with two huge oil discoveries in the North Sea and at Prudhoe Bay, Alaska, BP was inundated with crude oil. BP entered United States markets after purchasing from Atlantic Richfield the former Sinclair marketing along the eastern seaboard from Maine to Florida, along with some surplus Atlantic locations in the Northeast. BP signs were first erected at stations in this country in Atlanta, Georgia, in 1969.

Sohio had found its partner. In 1970, Sohio traded a minority interest with increases in ownership tied to crude oil production to British Petroleum in exchange for BP's U.S. marketing subsidiary BP Oil. The deal was mutually beneficial in that BP gained refinery capacity, access to pipelines, and a foothold in the huge U.S. gasoline market. Of the Sinclair locations it had purchased, many were old and poorly located. Sinclair had done little in the way of developing an interstate marketing

SOHIO
PUBLIC TELEPHONE
MANNERS
DRIVE IN
SOHIO SUPREME
SOHIO X-70
CONTAINS LEAD
SOHIO SUPREME
Polarine MOTOR OIL
BATTERY SERVICE
Polarine MOTOR OIL

This neon Sohio sign is now displayed in a private collection. ***Bruce Miller***

operation, preferring to brand small jobber-supplied stations on main street in every town east of the Rockies. By 1973, BP was in the process of selling off many of the stations and supply agreements in the Southeast, primarily to American Petrofina. Fina signs replaced BP signs at hundreds of stations. The remaining BP marketing network was within economical supply reach of Sohio refineries and pipelines. In one of the few market expansion moves by the company in the 1970s, Sohio purchased McLean, Virginia-based Scot Stations. Scot operated high-volume discount super pumpers in the Washington-Baltimore metropolitan area, as well as around Richmond and Norfolk. Successful outlets were eventually converted to the BP brand, although Sohio operated the Scot chain until the early 1980s. Also added to the Sohio retail presence was the Truckstops of America operation. TA, as it was commonly known, had seen several owners in the previous years, but with access to oil company reserves, both financially and product related, TA was finally in a position to solidify its place among the nation's truck stop operators.

As BP ownership in Sohio increased and Sohio's crude oil supply problems subsided, market expansion again became a corporate interest. When Chevron merged with Gulf in 1984, the Gulf marketing in the Southeast overlapped the existing Chevron marketing in the former Kyso states. To avoid antitrust action, the Gulf marketing in eight southeastern states, the stations and jobber supply contracts were sold to Sohio, with a license to use the Gulf logo for a minimum of five years. The beginning of 1985 found Sohio operating stations under

This collector recreates a Sohio scene from the past at an Ohio swap meet.

left
"The Sign of Service On Every Ohio Road" was the slogan that identified Sohio stations like this to postwar motorists. ***Joe and Judy Gross***

Sohio stations prominently displayed the "Standard Oil" name until BP rebranded the stations in 1991. This typical Sohio outlet was photographed in Elyria, Ohio, in 1990.

brands Sohio, Boron, BP, Scot, Wm. Penn, TA, Gulf, Gas and Go (a trademark introduced as a secondary brand at former Boron outlets in Michigan), and Gibbs (a New England jobber brand that BP had inherited as a secondary brand in the Sinclair purchase).

One hundred and seventeen years after John D. Rockefeller consolidated his petroleum operations into Cleveland, Ohio-based Standard Oil, his original operation known as Standard Oil Company of Ohio ceased to exist as a corporate entity. The year was 1987, and British Petroleum, exercising an option dating back to the original merger with Sohio, purchased the remaining portions of the company. Standard Oil Company of Ohio became BP America. Much speculation was made about the eventual choice of brand names to be used, particularly among Gulf jobbers and dealers in the Southeast. Gulf was the most well-respected brand in some parts of the South, and any change needed to be thought out carefully. Prior to 1987, Sohio had originally intended to eventually replace Gulf with Boron and had already expanded that brand into new territory with some Boron stations in Virginia. With the BP purchase in 1987, the plans changed as it became apparent that the BP brand, familiar only through its use on former Sinclair outlets, would replace not only Gulf, but Boron and the other brands as well. "Would the Sohio brand be spared?" was a question headlining several trade publications. Sohio, identified for more than sixty years with its homestate Ohio, had been, perhaps, the perfect gasoline trademark. Sohio stations were the most familiar commercial site in Ohio. If BP were to replace Sohio, would it have any lasting effects?

Nashville, Tennessee, was chosen as the test market for the new BP brand. Prior to this time, Gulf, Sohio, and Boron stations had received a reimaging, with station components fashioned from silver panels and the respective logos displayed on a

Assorted Sohio motor oil cans from the postwar era.

green background. In the summer of 1989, all Gulf outlets in Nashville and Davidson County, Tennessee, were converted to BP brand, and the complete BP image package was displayed to the buying public for the first time. Motorists reacted favorably, so beginning with a single station in Marshall, North Carolina, in May 1990, Gulf stations in eight states were converted to BP in five months of rebranding and reimaging. Atlas products, inherited by BP from Sohio, became available to former Gulf jobbers, who tended to remain strong in TBA items. Boron outlets and the other brands were converted to BP in 1990 as well. The following year, 1991, Ohio lost its namesake landmarks as the BP brand replaced Sohio, again in a summer rebranding and reimaging.

BP America, as a successor to Standard Oil Company of Ohio, is today a fully integrated unit of British Petroleum and ranks eighth in assets and ninth in number of stations, with nearly 7,000 branded outlets in twenty-seven states, including some West Coast stations where the BP brand was franchised to West Coast independent Tosco.

The Ohio Oil Company–USX/Marathon

The Ohio Oil Company served primarily as the production arm of the Standard Oil Trust. Founded in Lima, Ohio, in 1887, The Ohio, as it was commonly called, was organized by production companies in the Lima field in order to compete against the domination of Standard. Crude oil recovered from the Lima field was known to be high in sulfur content, but Standard purchased as much as could be bought, stockpiling it in anticipation of discovery of a process to refine the high-sulfur crude into usable products. In 1888, Standard entered into production in the Lima "Trenton Rock" (as it is sometimes known) oil fields through its National Transit subsidiary, a tank car operator. Within a year of this entry, The Ohio had sold out to Standard, a victim of the hold Standard had on transportation of crude oil. Production men from National Transit took control of The Ohio in April 1889, bringing with them one James Donnell, whose family would dominate The Ohio for most of the coming century. As refining techniques for high-sulfur crude were developed and put into place at Standard's huge Whiting, Indiana, refining complex, pipelines under Standard control were extended to the Trenton Rock fields to ease transportation of the crude to Standard refineries. The Ohio had no sales department and no customers, as it existed only to supply the great industrial machine that was Standard Oil. Offices of The Ohio, which had shifted to Oil City,

This 1941 map displays an artist's conception of the unique glass Marathon spinner sign with runner logo.

The Ohio Oil Company adopted the Marathon trademark when it purchased Transcontinental Oil in 1930. Shown here is an early Transcontinental Marathon sign.

Pennsylvania, when National Transit took over, were moved from Oil City in 1901 to Findlay, Ohio, the center of company production operations. By this time, Ohio had become the first state to investigate the holdings and dominance of Standard, the road leading to the eventual breakup of Standard in 1911 having begun in Columbus in 1898.

The Ohio, simply a small-town-based production subsidiary, was far removed from the day-to-day operation of Standard and from the forthcoming court battles. Its only job was to extract oil from the ground. When the separation of the Standard companies came in 1911, The Ohio was particularly vulnerable since it had only one customer. Left somewhat in limbo at the time of the breakup, The Ohio simply continued selling its crude to its former customers, other siblings in the Standard family. It was a stand-alone entity now, though, and worked hard to show a profit. Crude from The Ohio's wells was transported via pipelines owned by former siblings to refineries owned by the Standard companies from New Jersey, Indiana, and New York, as well as to Atlantic and lubricants refineries operated by Vacuum Oil. Indeed, The Ohio crude served most of the needs of Standard of New Jersey until 1919 when Jersey acquired Texas producer Humble Oil and became a major player in oil field development.

Transcontinental's Marathon runner appeared on pump globes of the 1920s as well as on station signs.

The Ohio looked west in the teens, for to survive as a production company exploration had to continue. The time always comes when a producing field plays out. The Ohio sought out oil aggressively in Wyoming, but success was slow in coming. By 1921, production in the Rockies was profitable, with many lessons learned. Oil production began in Kansas as well but using the method that would profit The Ohio greatly in years to come, that of buying existing production. This lesson was learned early, as the earliest years in Wyoming had been costly. Locating oil-producing property was a roll of the dice. In Kansas, The Ohio demonstrated it had learned the lesson well, and this time the company acquired production through the purchase of Mid Kansas Oil and Gas Company. Mid Kansas was one of many firms created by veteran oil men Michael Benedum and Joseph Trees. The partnership of Benedum and Trees was one that thrived on skill and luck,

The Marathon runner was modernized somewhat by the time this sign was introduced in 1946. ***Frank Regetti***

and as they were quick to jump from one venture to the next, The Ohio was never far behind to buy up the pieces. Simply put, Benedum and Trees took the risks. The Ohio bought in for the long haul and made it profitable. The partners would figure closely throughout much of The Ohio's history.

In 1924, The Ohio entered a new phase of its history with the purchase of Robinson, Illinois-based Lincoln Oil Refining Company. Lincoln Oil had been a bargain purchase and with it came a small chain of service stations, selling gasoline branded Linco in Indiana and Illinois. With this move, The Ohio became an integrated oil company, involved in production, transportation, refining, and finally, marketing. The Linco brand would be pushed into a larger and larger area around Robinson in the years to come, and by 1927 Linco gasoline was available in parts of Missouri, Iowa, Ohio, Kentucky, and Michigan as well. Learning a lesson from the production side of the business, the Linco brand expansion came through the purchase of numerous wholesale gasoline marketing companies, as markets such as Fort Wayne, Indiana, were entered with the purchase of Red Fox Oil Company in 1928. Red Fox stations and other acquisitions were branded Linco as quickly as possible, and the brand became well recognized throughout its territory.

Through Mid Kansas, The Ohio was able to avoid the laws prejudicial to former Standard companies in Texas and began to develop Texas production. This led to the development of the west Texas oil field known as Yates Field, the greatest oil discovery in the United States, in 1926. Once again, the partners Benedum and Trees entered the picture. In 1915, they had formed Riverside Oil Company, based in Pittsburgh, Pennsylvania, which later was absorbed by Transcontinental Oil, the entity created by the partners in 1920.

In 1924, Transcontinental and Mid Kansas entered into exploration of what became Yates Field in a partnership deal that, as usual, had Transcontinental absorbing much of the risk. The Yates development was largely a last effort for Transcontinental, though, and despite the success, the partners were quick to move on to their newest venture, Republic Oil Company. In 1930, The Ohio purchased, through Mid Kansas, Transcontinental Oil.

With Transcontinental came not only production but refining and marketing as well, and with the purchase, The Ohio—rather Mid Kansas—found itself supplying nearly 400 service

The Marathon M is displayed against a clear midwestern sky at Veedersburg, Indiana, in 1989.

This Marathon outlet in Illinois marked the transition between the Linco and Marathon trademarks in the East. It's shown here in 1942.

stations with a product branded Marathon throughout the Midwest and South. The Marathon brand got its name from ancient Greek history and the legend of the great battle at the plains of Marathon, where Grecian armies were victorious over Persian forces intent on winning. Marathon's symbol was a running man, Pheidippides, who carried news of the Greek victory to Athens in a sprint that was commemorated as a "Marathon" run. The name and trademark were one of the most distinctive in the petroleum industry, and The Ohio continued to use it. Stations in the East remained as Linco for the time being, while stations in the Midwest and South carried the proud name of Marathon.

This, in essence, begins the modern era for the Ohio Oil Company. The Depression saw a company that was involved in crude oil production throughout the Midwest; in natural gas production in Wyoming; in crude transportation; in refining through Lincoln Oil at Robinson, Illinois, and through Transcontinental at Boynton, Oklahoma, and Bristow and Ft. Worth, Texas; and in marketing under the Linco and Marathon trademarks throughout the Midwest. The Ohio was a fully integrated oil company in every sense of the word. In 1934, Mid Kansas was reorganized as the Marathon Oil Company subsidiary. The following year properties of Lincoln Oil Refining were completely absorbed into The Ohio, and in 1936 properties of Marathon were absorbed as well, paving the way for a unified refining and marketing structure. Gradually, in the era from 1936 to 1939, the Marathon trademark, now revised into traditional red-white-and-blue colors from Transcontinental's green and orange, replaced the Linco brand in Ohio, Michigan, Kentucky, Indiana, and Illinois. Still, the corporation suffered somewhat from name recognition, as "The Ohio" was known as a crude oil production firm, while the Marathon name gave no indication of corporate ownership.

World War II saw The Ohio providing aviation fuels to the war effort and the elimination of the far-flung Marathon marketing territory. With supply problems at best, the distant markets

This prewar Marathon prototype was constructed in Springfield, Illinois, in 1940.

were abandoned to concentrate on those areas—Illinois, Indiana, Kentucky, Ohio, and Michigan—that could be served by the Robinson refinery. Marathon marketing farther west, the heart of the old Transcontinental area, was sold off to Tidewater-Associated, and stations were rebranded Tydol Flying A. With this sale, it was apparent that profits, not gallonage and sales volume, had become the company's focus. It was one that would serve The Ohio well in the coming years.

The early postwar years was a time of image enhancement for The Ohio. The famed Marathon trademark was revised for easier recognition, and new station prototypes were introduced. Quality jobber representation was solicited, and the gaps in the marketing area were filled. Still, the Marathon brand remained one that was seen primarily in small towns and in the new suburban strips that were developing. That would soon change, as in 1958, The Ohio purchased Cincinnati-based Tower Oil Company and established the Marathon brand firmly in Cincinnati and surrounding suburbs. The following year, 1959, The Ohio purchased Detroit-based Aurora Oil Company. Founded in 1930, Aurora marketed the Speedway 79 brand in Michigan, primarily in Detroit and surrounding areas. The purchase put The Ohio firmly in major markets for the first time in its existence, although once again, the company

The Marathon "blue brick" design featured an illuminated facade and was adopted by Marathon from Speedway when Marathon purchased the company in 1959. *Dick Doumanian*

Shown here is the Speedway version of the "blue brick" station. ***Dick Doumanian***

found itself with two distinct brands and marketing organizations, each well respected within its marketing territories. While Marathon began a phase out of the Speedway 79 brand three years after the 1959 purchase, the name would rise again into prominence many years later in today's gasoline market.

Replacement of the Speedway brand with Marathon was done in conjunction with a complete reimaging of the company, indeed, even a corporate name change. For in 1962, The Ohio abandoned its corporate name of seventy-five years to take the name most familiar to the public, Marathon Oil. The famed Pheidippides trademark was retired as well, and in its place a large red M in an elongated blue hexagon became the company's trademark. It would replace the Pheidippides "Best In the Long Run" trademark, as well as the Speedway 79 brand in Michigan. The logo, designed for easy recognition at highway speeds, would serve the company well for many years to come.

The same year that the trademark Marathon was selected to identify the company, a final acquisition from the old partnership was made. In 1923, partners Michael Benedum and Joseph Trees founded Pittsburgh-based Republic Oil, primarily a refiner-marketer operating under the Republic shield trademark from New York to Florida. By 1962, both partners had passed away, and Republic, now known as Plymouth Oil, was for sale. Republic had sufficient domestic production to supply its refinery on the Texas Gulf Coast and product terminals throughout the Southeast, a large wholesale market and a network of branded jobbers that had been with Republic since the 1930s. It was new ground for Marathon, of a sort, since Marathon had been represented in these parts of the country some twenty to twenty-five years earlier. The brand remained Republic into the 1980s, and marketing was conducted separately from Marathon's primary territory and brand names. By the early 1980s, only a small number of branded jobbers remained, and the brand expired as a semblance of image requirements disappeared. Even today, as the Republic terminal network supplies Speedway/Starvin Marvin stores, you can still see an occasional

Republic Pow'r Pak'd or Hi-T decal on otherwise unbranded pumps in Virginia, North and South Carolina, and Georgia.

Marathon solidified its retail position in the 1960s, reaching a comfort level in major markets while retaining its loyal jobber and customer base in small towns. Branded marketing was restricted to five states—Ohio, Indiana, Illinois, Michigan, and Kentucky—with one interesting exception. While many oil companies created station networks along the nation's growing number of interstate highways, Marathon was the only one to attempt to expand from its home territory by centering on only one highway—Interstate 75 south. The logic was that Marathon customers in the five states would remain loyal to the brand on their frequent trips to Florida if stations were spaced at intervals along the major north-south corridor. Marathon signs appeared in such unlikely places as Clinton, Tennessee, and Rome, Georgia, at interstate locations only. Marathon maintained this unusual market expansion into Tennessee, Georgia, and Florida until the 1970s gas shortages shook brand loyalty in ways from which no brand has ever fully recovered.

The gas shortage brought another innovation to Marathon, and the company went to its own history book to select a name and image. As the gas shortage drug on, many longtime dealers tired of the hassles and gave up. Empty stations dotted the landscape. Marathon had good locations, but too few dealers elected to enter the retail trade directly. In order not to appear in competition with their dealers, these company-operated stations were branded Speedway. Many were nothing more than rows of gas pumps with a cashier's booth under a canopy. These were easily built at locations where station buildings were torn down. At other locations, service bays were boarded up, and "gas only" stations supplemented their existence

The Speedway trademark was reintroduced in the 1970s and today graces this truck stop at Corbin, Kentucky.

by sales of soft drinks and cigarettes. Mini-stores were born. The retail effort was extremely successful, and Marathon went shopping for chains of stations to buy in those areas where supply networks existed. First, in 1971, came Cleveland, Ohio-based Gastown, with dozens of stations in northeastern Ohio. Then in 1972, Oshkosh, Wisconsin-based Consolidated was added to the collection. The retail network was growing. In 1975, Marathon acquired Springfield, Ohio-based Bonded, a company with an innovative history in gasoline marketing.

In the fall of 1981, Marathon met its greatest challenge of the decade when another former Standard sibling, Mobil Oil, attempted to purchase the company. Fearing that Mobil was seeking only proven reserves, with no intention of keeping Marathon as an intact entity, Marathon executives and employees, even the citizens of towns where Marathon had operations, rose up in protest of the proposed buyout. Marathon executives fought back, attempting a merger with some other company on more favorable terms. Non-oil industrial companies were scouted, and when no solid leads ensued, other oil companies were considered, notably Gulf Oil. Less than three weeks after Mobil first announced the takeover attempt, Pittsburgh-based U.S. Steel was the new owner of Marathon. In a restructuring that followed, U.S. Steel became USX, and Marathon was the largest and most profitable component of the new entity. Although Marathon Oil officially ceased to exist in 1981, USX continues to this day to be dominated by Marathon. All petroleum operations were consolidated as USX subsidiary Marathon Oil, as the company is still identified.

The merger only heightened the need for downstream operations to get closer to the consumer. Marathon continued to purchase regional gas station chains as it had in the 1970s. Next came a joint investment with Exxon in Chicago-based Cheker. Cheker had been founded in 1968 from several smaller chain operations and was one of the most successful discounters in the Chicago market. As Exxon withdrew from the upper Midwest, its interest in Cheker, and an affiliate that used the reincarnated Oklahoma brand on some former Exxon outlets, lessened and Marathon purchased the balance of the operation in September 1983. By this time, Cheker had also purchased St. Louis-based Imperial Refineries, an old-time discounter that at one time had been a mid-continent refiner-marketer. Imperial was a far-flung operation, with stations throughout the Midwest and South. Those locations that could not be supported by Marathon's existing product distribution system were abandoned, and locations in the South were converted to the Ecol brand after Marathon purchased Jackson, Mississippi-based Ecol in May 1984. By this time, Marathon had also purchased Greenville, South Carolina-based Webster Service Stations, operating under the Value brand in North and South Carolina.

In 1984, the Speedway brand had appeared at a few stations formerly bearing some of these purchased brand names, primarily in the area associated with the Consolidated stations. The entire secondary brand markets were grouped under the corporate subsidiary, Emro Marketing, Emro meaning "Marathon Retail Operations." Indeed, the Emro stations were a retail operation as opposed to an oil company. Local brands were preserved to the extent possible. The next expansion came in late 1984 when Charleston, South Carolina-based Port Oil Company was added to the operation. Then, in 1985, Emro purchased Chamblee, Georgia-based Globe Oil Company. Globe operated the Starvin Marvin convenience stores in Georgia and the Carolinas. Their highway locations were valuable additions to the Emro operation, whose other stations were high-volume outlets but concentrated in locations other than interstate interchanges. The Starvin Marvin brand name was an important acquisition as well, as it was chosen as the convenience store name for all the Emro outlets. The Starvin Marvin name was teamed with a revised Speedway logo, and many of the Emro outlets were reimaged with the Speedway/Starvin Marvin signage and graphics. Former Marathon dealer outlets in advantageous locations were converted to Speedway/Starvin Marvin outlets as their leases were up.

A typical assortment of Marathon and affiliated brand cans.

Marathon's next significant addition came in 1989 with the purchase of Indianapolis, Indiana-based Rock Island Refining. Rock Island had been founded before World War II in Oklahoma, and the operation had shifted to Indiana after the war. It was a major supplier of unbranded gasoline to discounters and began buying up some of its customers, including Golden Imperial, Colonial-Progressive, and Tulsa, in the 1970s. Its biggest purchase was Indianapolis-based United in 1985, and most of the other Rock Island stations were rebranded United. When Marathon purchased the Rock Island refinery, its retail marketing was assigned to Emro as well. Marathon continued to operate the refinery until 1993.

Other purchases in the mid-1990s include another Rock Island-supplied Indianapolis marketer, Wake Up. Wake Up was the brand used by J. A. Hogshire and Company, which operated several dozen stations throughout Indiana. Also added to the collection were the Indiana and Illinois locations belonging to Martin Oil Service. Originally, Martin was a 1930s trackside operator that had split into several family factions in the 1950s. After expanding coast-to-coast in the 1960s, the operation was greatly curtailed in the gas shortages of the 1970s. The high-volume outlets were converted to Speedway, while several retain the Martin brand as of this writing.

As the retail side of Marathon, Emro, evolved, the branded operation was not neglected. The Marathon brand expanded into southern Wisconsin and into West Virginia by the mid-1980s. In 1992, Marathon began soliciting jobbers in those areas of Virginia, Tennessee, and North Carolina that could be economically served from existing terminals. Today, the Marathon brand appears on nearly 2,400 stations in eleven states while the various Emro brands appear on more than 1,600 stations in sixteen states. (Speedway is the dominant brand, but the outcry of petroleum collectibles hobbyists in 1990 slowed the efforts to rebrand, and many locations retain their original brand.) Today the USX/Marathon subsidiary ranks tenth in assets among oil companies and eleventh in profitability, with nearly $11 million in assets.

The Atlantic Refining Company–Atlantic Richfield Company

The Atlantic Refining Company was founded in Philadelphia in 1866 as the Atlantic Petroleum Storage Company, operating a refined products river terminal on the Philadelphia waterfront. The company engaged in wholesaling refined products, buying on the open market and reselling to retail establishments. Competition from refiners dealing directly with retailers or the public prompted Atlantic to construct its own refinery. In 1870, the company was reorganized as the Atlantic Refining Company, the name by which it would be known for most of the next century. The origins of Atlantic Refining correspond exactly to those of Standard Oil, and the success of Atlantic did not escape the notice of the Rockefeller interests. Continuing the practice of purchasing successful companies, or anything else that might get in the way, Standard purchased Atlantic Refining in 1874.

This 1931 Atlantic map includes Atlantic's original marketing territory and its earliest expansion areas.

With access to Standard money, Atlantic began the most significant expansion the company had seen to date. The Philadelphia refinery and terminal was greatly enlarged, becoming one of the most important petroleum facilities in eastern Pennsylvania and one of Philadelphia's largest employers. Work began on a Pittsburgh refinery, whose location, in close proximity to the Pennsylvania oil region, proved to be of great significance. By the early

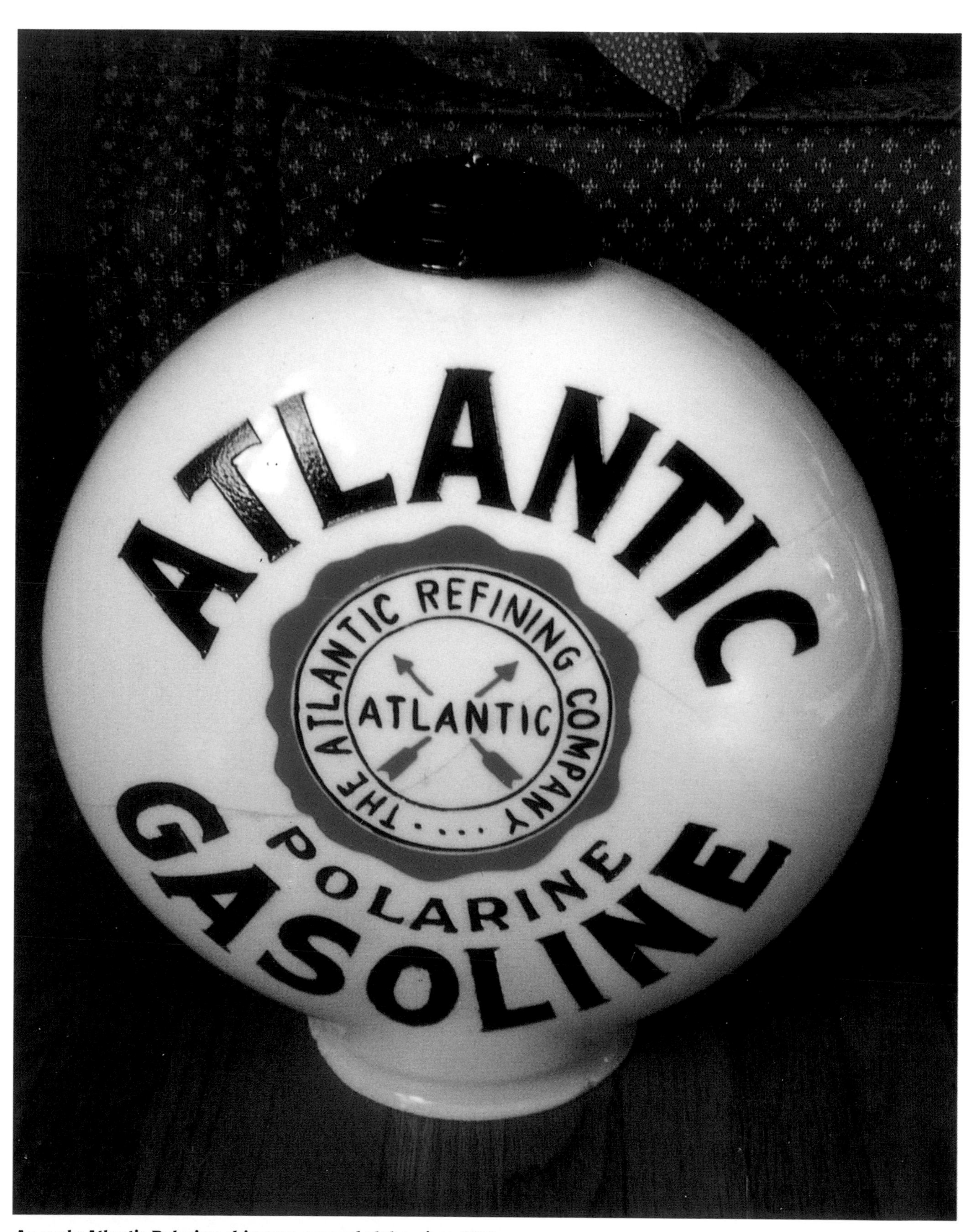

An early Atlantic Polarine chimney-capped globe, circa 1916.

A typical Atlantic sign and elaborate metalworking of a pole structure from the 1930s.

1890s, all of Standard's refining and marketing properties in Pennsylvania and Delaware had been consolidated into Atlantic Refining. The Standard years were good to Atlantic. The company's kerosene, and later gasoline, was heavily promoted. Atlantic became involved in lubricants in this era as well, developing the automotive oil Polarine, one of the trademarks that would become a property of contention after the breakup of Standard. Virtually all of the Standard marketers used the Polarine trademark after the 1911 breakup. Standard of Indiana continued the product in its line-up until 1961. Atlantic also marketed its gasoline under the Polarine trademark, the only one of the Standard companies to do so.

With the breakup of Standard in 1911, Atlantic found itself in much the same position that the other refiner-marketer siblings did: they had very little crude to refine. Atlantic scrambled as did the others, although they chose to explore for crude rather than buy up existing crude oil-producing companies. In the years between 1911 and 1920, Atlantic was successful in production in Kentucky, Texas, Arkansas, and Louisiana. Atlantic began branded marketing of gasoline in 1915, adopting an architectural style similar to that of Greek or Roman temples for a chain of service stations in Philadelphia. All marketing in the early era was handled directly, and gasoline filling stations were established in conjunction with existing bulk plants throughout Pennsylvania and in Delaware. Expansion began into New York, New Jersey, and New England by 1918, and into Maryland, Virginia, and the Carolinas in the early 1920s. In 1921, Atlantic opened a new refinery outside Brunswick, Georgia, to supply an ever-expanding market for refined products. By the middle 1920s, Atlantic began actively soliciting jobbers, one of the first companies to adopt this method of operation, and turned the operation of virtually all of its service stations over to independent dealers.

Atlantic was also one of the first domestic oil companies to establish a significant marketing presence overseas. Atlantic had turned to its origins for direction and, taking a lesson from the company's founders, began supplying products to growing Asian markets. The Atlantic brand was known in Europe as well, as many of

Atlantic's products were sold by other Standard affiliates in Europe prior to the breakup. One marketing outpost that proved most successful was Brazil.

By 1930, Atlantic was marketing in thirteen eastern seaboard states and inland as far west as eastern Ohio. With growing overseas markets, adequate refinery capacity, and an ever-growing number of successful production properties, Atlantic had overcome the obstacles in existence at the time of the breakup to become a successful, well-rounded company. During the 1930s, Atlantic was content to market its gasolines, Atlantic White Flash and Hi-Arc, and motor oils, Atlantic A Quality and Atlantic Aviation. Service station design was enlarged and standardized, a porcelain prototype being developed that would serve the company well, with slight modifications, for the next thirty years.

During World War II, Atlantic joined the rest of the petroleum industry in developing better aviation fuels for military use, as well as specialty lubricants necessary for wartime industries. After the war, Atlantic campaigned to upgrade stations and began building company-owned stations in major markets for lease to independent dealers. The company concentrated on neighborhood stations in these markets, Atlantic stations becoming a friendly place where local children could get air for bicycle tires and dad could get reliable automobile service. Service station dealers were encouraged to get involved in local delivery of home heating oil, and many stations added additional storage, in effect creating mini bulk plants. Atlantic increased station construction in Florida, a popular winter retreat for its core customers in northern markets, and in Virginia, building its neighborhood stations in the suburban residential areas of military towns such as Norfolk and Newport News and the growing Northern Virginia/D.C. area. The outdated and unusual product names White Flash and Hi Arc were replaced in 1952 by Atlantic and Atlantic Premium. Atlantic Premium became Atlantic Imperial in 1957.

To a certain extent, and in spite of its expansion-based marketing philosophy, Atlantic as a company stagnated. Although some foreign exploration was attempted, Atlantic remained very much a domestic company. World War II had

The Atlantic brand returned in the 1980s as Arco sold eastern marketing to an independent who adopted the name. Shown here is the newest of two logos from the "new" Atlantic.

taken many of Atlantic's overseas marketing outlets, and in a sense, Atlantic retreated into what it did best, refine domestic crude and push it through a network of service stations. The stagnation did not escape the attention of the company's largest stockholder, though. Robert Anderson had become Atlantic's largest stockholder in 1962 by

A porcelain Atlantic station at Greenville, South Carolina, in 1952. The pylon tower was typical of stations in the postwar era.

trading his crude production operation in the Southwest to Atlantic in a stock exchange. He had previously been very successful in his investment in Wilshire Oil, a California refiner-marketer purchased by Gulf in the late 1950s. In 1965, Anderson, in his position as largest stockholder, became involved in the management of the company. Recognizing the need to solidify more crude production capacity and to diversify from East Coast markets that had been hard hit in gasoline price wars in the early 1960s, Atlantic began efforts to purchase the Pure Oil Company and, unsuccessful in its bid, turned to Richfield Oil Corporation of California.

Richfield Oil Corporation had been founded in the early years of this century as a pioneer in California oil production. It began gasoline marketing before 1920 and rapidly became a major player in California markets. In 1929, it purchased New York-based Walburn Oil Company and from Walburn's holdings established Richfield Oil Company of New York. Richfield of New York was primarily a marketer, an all-jobber company that owned no stations but supplied products and a brand to reputable jobbers from Maine to Florida. Richfield overextended itself in the early 1930s and entered bankruptcy proceedings. Rescued from receivership by Sinclair, and to a lesser extent Cities Service, Richfield was reorganized as an independent integrated company in 1937. Sinclair had purchased the Richfield of New York operation outright in 1935, and from that time until the New York company was dissolved and merged into Sinclair in 1964, the two remained separate companies entirely, all the while sharing a brand name, image, colors, and heritage. This arrangement causes much confusion among students of the petroleum industry today.

Atlantic began merger negotiations with Richfield in late 1965, and the two companies merged in January 1966 to form Atlantic Richfield Company. The merger created a much stronger company than either Atlantic or Richfield could ever have hoped to become on their own. Before the end of 1966, the company began identifying itself as Arco, although gas stations retained their respective Atlantic or Richfield identification. Topping the list of priorities for the new organization, the company concentrated on improving its position in domestic oil production, and in 1968 discovered oil on Alaska's north shore, the most significant domestic oil development in history. Alaska took Arco into the big leagues among petroleum companies. Arco had discovered so much oil that it brought in partners, including BP, to assist in developing the field and creating a transportation infrastructure necessary to bring the oil from the frozen North to existing crude terminals and refineries.

Assorted Atlantic pump signs from the 1950s and '60s.

Atlantic motor oil cans from the 1930s through 1970.

Arco was no longer content to rest on its success. In 1970, it purchased Sinclair Oil, the most significant oil industry merger in history until that time. Sinclair, founded in 1916 from the various production and refining holdings of oil pioneer Harry Sinclair, was a fully integrated company with domestic production, pipeline, and other transportation facilities, refineries, and branded service stations in most states east of the Rockies. Sinclair still controlled a significant interest in Richfield prior to the Atlantic-Richfield merger and appeared to be an excellent addition to the Arco organization. The U.S. Justice Department thought it may have been too good an opportunity and ordered Arco to sell Sinclair holdings in the East, where they overlapped with existing Atlantic holdings. Arco sold the Sinclair refinery, terminals, and service station network to its Alaska partner, BP, in 1970. With the purchase, Atlantic, Richfield, and Sinclair stations began rebranding to Arco, the corporate acronym that had been in use since the merger. Atlantic and Richfield stations were rebranded first, but before Sinclair stations could be rebranded, the Justice Department announced it was still not satisfied with the arrangement. Arco was court ordered to sell the Sinclair marketing in the Midwest, and in 1973 the properties were spun off to form the new Sinclair Oil Corporation which operates nearly 2,800 stations today in twenty-two midwestern and Rocky Mountain states. At this time, Arco also announced that it was withdrawing from marketing in the Southeast, and jobber contracts in the Carolinas, Georgia, and Florida were not renewed. Company stations in these areas were closed in record numbers or sold to former jobbers who wanted them, the jobbers themselves being pinched for supply during the first of the 1970s gas shortages.

By 1980, Arco had begun converting many of its remaining locations in the Northeast and on the West Coast to Arco AM/PM convenience stores, a concept it had adopted from several successful independents. Arco's stores were among the first operated by major oil companies and proved particularly successful in metropolitan areas such as Washington, D.C., and Los Angeles. Corporate headquarters had shifted to Los Angeles in 1972, and Arco was very much a western company in scope as well as philosophy. In 1985, Arco withdrew from the last of its eastern Atlantic markets and the Northeast. Arco sold locations in New England to Shell, and in New York and Pennsylvania to a new refiner-marketing entity, named appropriately enough Atlantic Refining. Fifteen years after Arco signs had replaced Atlantic signs in New York and Pennsylvania, the Arco signs came down, and Atlantic signs went up. The convenience stores that had proved so successful to Arco were renamed Atlantic A-Plus stores, and the new marketer was well on its way to success. In 1988, Atlantic Refining became a wholly owned subsidiary of Sun Oil, although Atlantic marketing remained separate from Sunoco marketing until 1994.

Meanwhile, Arco concentrated all its marketing efforts on the former Richfield territory on the West Coast, creating an extensive network of company-owned and operated Arco AM/PM stores. Arco took an aggressive pricing stance, becoming, in effect, a discounter, determined to sell gasoline at lower prices using fewer frills. Arco became a leader in California's efforts to minimize pollution from automobile exhaust as well, introducing cleaner-burning gasolines and refitting refineries to produce each generation of mandated "reformulated" gasolines. Arco's discounter marketing concept was maintained until the mid-1990s, when Arco began retrenching in some markets and pricing more in line with other major oil companies operating on the West Coast. Today the Arco brand appears on only about 1,600 stations in five far western states. Despite the greatly diminished marketing structure, Arco ranks seventh in assets among oil companies, with more than $24 billion in corporate assets.

Continental Oil Company–Conoco, Inc.

Conoco today is the least "Standard" of the Standard siblings. Some would tell you that Conoco ceased to exist in 1929 when Marland Oil Company purchased the Continental Oil Company, choosing to retain the Continental name and Conoco trademark. Others would tell you that Conoco ceased to exist when it was purchased by DuPont in 1982, becoming a DuPont subsidiary. Whatever the view of Continental's corporate status today, no one can doubt Conoco's heritage and its contributions to the petroleum industry. The Conoco brand is the oldest of the primary brand names used by any of the Standard affiliates.

Stated simply, Continental brought petroleum products to the Rocky Mountains. In the sparsely settled land of the Rockies, refined petroleum products were something of a luxury before Continental Oil was founded in Ogden, Utah, in 1875. Although incorporated in Iowa, Ogden served as the first business and distribution center for Conoco's petroleum-trading operations. Kerosene and lubricants were the primary products of that day, and the emerging cities of the Rockies, particularly Denver, became important markets for Continental's products. Looking farther west, Continental was established in California as a petroleum products manufacturer before 1880 and was involved in the founding of a crude production company in 1879, Pacific Coast Oil, which later evolved into Standard of California.

Conoco operated "America's foremost free motor travel service," as indicated on this 1935 map that was given away as part of the Conoco Travel Bureau.

A classic Conoco station in Hampton, Virginia, 1938.

Pipeline transportation of petroleum products was important in the company's early years as well, considering Continental's efforts at marketing over a large and sparsely settled area. Continental was among the first to offer local tank wagon delivery as well, establishing bulk plants at strategic points and basing horsedrawn tank wagons there for customers over an extended local area.

Continental's business functions as a petroleum products trader seem rather mundane until you consider that it was operating in what, at the time, was actually hostile territory. An early bulk facility was established at Billings, Montana, in 1876, the same year that Custer lost at Little Big Horn. All of Conoco's early expansion was largely driven through the ambition of the founder, Isaac Blake. By 1880, Blake's Continental Oil was the most significant competition to Standard Oil in the West. As Standard had done with all other competitors of significance, it began negotiating to purchase Continental. The deal was made in late 1884, and as of January 1885, Continental became an operating unit of Standard Oil.

This Baltimore 1940 prototype was typical of Conoco stations built in the East just prior to World War II.

This alliance gave Standard its first significant marketing presence in the western plains and the Rockies. Standard's experience with the established bulk plant network and tank wagon delivery system was later adopted by Standard of Indiana and in actuality paved the way for today's refined petroleum distribution system. Continental was free to expand as a petroleum transportation and trading company, no longer having to search for crude to refine or worry about refineries to maintain. In this era, Conoco did acquire a minority interest in a Colorado refining company, which it finally completed the purchase of in 1916, after the breakup when refining independence had become a necessity. Conoco was not deeply involved in production during the Standard era but did continue to develop drilling equipment and practices from its early days on the West Coast. Potential crude production was passed along to other Standard siblings more heavily involved in exploration.

Today's Conoco owes much of its heritage to Marland Oil.

With the merger of Conoco and Marland in 1929, the company took on Marland's triangle logo and Conoco's brand name.

As a marketing company, kerosene remained Continental's primary product, but after 1900 there were more and more calls at Conoco plants for gasoline. Originally a waste product and later a stove fuel, gasoline was gaining popularity as a motor fuel for the newly developed automobiles. Such machines were still scarce in the plains and Rockies, though, and kerosene would dominate the product mix until after 1910. After Continental emerged from the breakup of Standard in 1911, the corporate entity was reorganized in Denver as the Continental Oil Company. Simply a marketing firm, Conoco began construction of a network of filling stations in Denver in 1915. The continental soldier standing at attention became the corporate trademaker, and the company's products were sold under the acronym brand name Conoco. In 1916, as noted above, Conoco completed the purchase of United Oil Company, giving it total control of a Colorado refinery and access to crude production in the Rockies. Marketing continued to dominate, though, as the filling station network expanded throughout the West. Franchised stations inside Yellowstone National Park were established in this era as well, a marketing arrangement that continues to this day.

Conoco re-entered markets in the East in 1959 with the purchase of Chattanooga-based Kayo. Children loved the candy-striped Kayo stations.

Meanwhile, in 1917, Marland Oil Company was consolidated from the various holdings of oil exploration pioneer E. W. Marland. Marland's production fields were primarily in Oklahoma, and headquarters for the company was at Ponca City. Make no mistake about it, Marland was an oil production firm, similar in functions to Oklahoma neighbors of the era, Phillips and Skelly. Marland began gasoline marketing in 1920, though, using an inverted red triangle with "Marland Oils" superimposed across the center as a marketing logo. It was a trademark that would appear in various forms over the next fifty years. Marland's triangle appeared across the Midwest and eventually along the East Coast after Marland purchased several gasoline marketers in New York and New Jersey. The Morgan banking interests invested heavily in Marland by the middle 1920s, and by 1928, Mr. Marland had lost control of the company, in lean times, to the Morgan interests. Selected to lead Marland was a former Texaco executive, Dan Moran, who proved to be very much a hands-on manager. Expansion ever on his mind and backed by Morgan money, one of Moran's first acts was for Marland to acquire Baltimore-based Prudential Refining, further expanding Marland's base in the more profitable, densely populated East Coast. Early in 1929, Moran began negotiations with Denver-based Continental to acquire the assets of that company. The Marland-Continental merger took place on April 30, 1929, and although it was basically a buyout of Continental by Marland, the surviving entity bore the Continental Oil name. In effect, Continental Oil, descendant of the Standard Oil Trust, ceased to exist. What survived was a renamed Marland. The Conoco trademark replaced "Marland Oils" across the famed red triangle logo, and it was displayed at service stations across thirty states, from New York and Georgia to Washington and New Mexico.

The modern era of Conoco essentially begins with the merger, and the surviving company is only tied to the original through heritage and name. The marketing style was dominated by Marland men, and in Continental Oil tradition as a marketer, Conoco quickly became a successful gasoline marketer. Numerous special services were offered to the motoring public, coordinated largely through the Conoco Travel Bureau. Conoco became the first gasoline marketer to promote pleasure travel, realizing that pleasure travel could contribute the most significant amount of new business of any function that could be addressed. Tourists took to the many services offered as part of the Conoco Travel Bureau, and in the years before World War II, Conoco's organization ranked second only to AAA in terms of tourist services. Also during the 1930s, Conoco heavily promoted its lubricants, specifically Germ Processed and Nth Motor oils, distributing them over an area much larger than where Conoco operated service stations.

World War II interrupted, and wartime restrictions on travel were naturally felt by a company that was so heavily dependent upon

Conoco high-rise signage is seen here against the Colorado sky.

Conoco adopted its European brand name, Jet, for secondary operations in the United States in 1980. Shown here is a Jet station on State Street in Bristol, Tennessee.

tourism. Aviation gasoline production and specialty lubricants helped make up the difference in sales, and Conoco became a leader in these fields, supplying the war effort with these much needed petroleum products. Following the war, Conoco was well positioned to take advantage of the surge in tourist travel, and the Conoco Travel Bureau again figured into the company's success in this era. In 1950, Conoco celebrated its seventy-fifth year of operation, introducing a revised red triangle logo in conjunction with the event. Also in 1950, Conoco completed the transfer of marketing properties in the East to the lease operation of Cities Service. Conoco stations, bulk plants, and terminals from New York to Georgia were leased long-term, and Conoco jobbers in those areas rebranded to Cities Service. This marked Conoco's first move in concentrating marketing in those areas where the company could be most self-sufficient and recreated the image of the "western" company, a theme Conoco would continue to use to the present with its "Hottest Brand Going" slogan. Not content to be sacrificing marketing areas for lack of supply, Conoco began seeking an ever-increasing amount of self-sufficiency in crude production, leading Conoco to involvement in a huge oil discovery in Libya in the late 1950s. Conoco entered the big leagues of international oil companies with this discovery and, supplies assured, could resume marketing expansion.

The late 1950s expansion came in a different form than earlier efforts. Conoco chose to purchase existing marketing firms, actually so-called "discounters" or "price marketers," and continue its operation as if nothing had happened. Purchased in 1959 were Minneapolis-based Western Oil and Fuel, originators of the Husky trademark and operators of stations under the Western, Mileage, DS, and Zephyr brands. Each had its own significant history, except Western, which had only been introduced that year for the company's branded convenience stores, Western's answer to its

Conoco motor oil cans from the 1930s through 1970.

Minneapolis neighbors, Erickson and its Holiday and SuperAmerica convenience stores. Also added was Chattanooga-based F. P. Kendall and Company, operators of the red-and-white, candy-striped Kayo stations in the Southeast. Kayo was purely a discounter, one of the South's most successful, and the candy-striped above-ground tanks and sign poles made the stations a favorite of children everywhere. Both of these operations continued much as they had before, as did California-based Douglas Oil, which Conoco purchased in 1961. Retail marketing for these companies included Conoco motor oils. Lubricants remained a strong item for Conoco.

New station designs were incorporated in the 1960s, efforts to beautify the American roadside. By the late 1960s, the Mileage and DS brand names were replaced by Conoco, although the Western convenience stores continued under the Western brand, carving out enough of the market share to prove that the convenience-store concept was a viable business opportunity. In 1970, the famed red triangle, at the time one of the oldest gasoline logos in use, was replaced by a capsule-shaped trademark that continues in use today. Conoco stations of the era offered blending of fuels, making four grades ranging from subregular to super-premium available. The requirements for an unleaded product in the 1970s would eliminate this feature in time, but it was successful in the 1960s when compact cars competed with land schooners and each required the appropriate fuel.

Conoco survived the 1970s gas shortages relatively intact, taking advantage of the situation to eliminate marginal, nonprofitable stations. The convenience store experience through Western gave the company experience in this new field for major oil companies when postshortage stations needed

Conoco motor oil cans displaying the new logo after 1970.

something different. Conoco's Western stations and much of the Kayo marketing, emphasizing convenience stores, was rebranded Jet in 1980, taking the name from a company purchased in England in 1961. Conoco stations, primarily operated through branded jobbers, did not make the conversion quite as quickly; but by the early 1980s, many marketers were experimenting with their own stores as well.

In 1982, first former Standard sibling, Mobil Oil, and Canadian distiller Seagram's began purchasing Conoco stock in an effort to acquire control of the company. Other potential buyers saw the ease with which Seagram's had moved in and began a stock-grab themselves. The victor, chosen by Conoco as most compatible, was chemical giant DuPont. Conoco would give DuPont a retailing presence that it had never had, and Conoco's petroleum reserves would give DuPont further opportunities in various petrochemical products fields. The DuPont-Conoco arrangement has been a very successful union, and today Conoco is a thriving integrated oil company that just happens to be owned by a chemical giant.

Conoco's operations today, if separated from DuPont, would rank it eleventh in assets, with nearly $12 billion, among major oil companies. The company markets through more than 5,000 branded stations in thirty-seven states, including many former Jet stations branded to Conoco in the South. Conoco has aggressively moved into the Southeast again, with Conoco signs appearing alongside the highways of Virginia, the Carolinas, and Georgia for the first time in more than forty years. A marketing tie-in with Utah-based Flying J, a national truck stop operator, has placed Conoco signs at gasoline facilities at its truck stops nationwide, and the Conoco capsule appears in many places the company's founders could have never envisioned.

South Penn Oil Company–Pennzoil, Inc.

This 1936 Pennzip map ties the familiar Pennzoil brand to the new Pennzip brand. Note distribution by a Dayton, Ohio, jobber.

Pennsylvania-grade crude oil has long been prized by refiners for having the characteristics necessary for refining the world's best lubricants. The term "Pennsylvania grade" applies to all crude produced in the oil region that extends from Western New York, through Pennsylvania and Ohio and extending south into West Virginia. With the formation of the Pennsylvania Grade Crude Oil Association (PGCOA) in 1924, any lubricant claiming to be Pennsylvania grade, from 1926 (when the licensing procedure was instituted) to the present, must be licensed by the association.

In 1889, the same year Standard purchased the Ohio Oil Company and entered the oil exploration and production fields, South Penn Oil Company was created by Standard to serve as an exploration and production operation in Pennsylvania, with the specific directive to develop the southern most reaches of the Pennsylvania oil regions, located mostly in West Virginia. The move served to solidify Standard's crude production position, and Standard's orderly methods of operation again proved to be the fabled Angel of Mercy to Pennsylvania oil producers, who had long been susceptible to wild price fluctuations.

A rare and beautiful Pennzoil globe from the early 1920s.

Three years prior to the founding of South Penn, a group of investors had joined together and constructed a refinery for kerosene production just outside Oil City, Pennsylvania. The new entity operated under the name Penn Refining Company. In 1893, South Penn joined forces with another refiner operating on an adjacent tract of land, Germania Refining. The two refineries produced high-quality kerosene and some gasoline for use in stoves and lighting equipment of that day. As the automobile age dawned, Penn Refining and Germania established a lubricants blending plant and began the manufacture of high-quality motor oils and greases. Product output from the two operations was sold on the wholesale market quite successfully. Packaged

A typical small town Pennzip station from the late 1930s.

under several different retailer's trademarks, the lubricants were well respected in the marketplace. The success of the wholesale distribution operation led several of the partners in the refining operations to establish a retail marketing company in 1909. The new company, Oil City Oil and Grease Company, trademarked the lubricant Merit.

In 1913, the management of Oil City Oil and Grease saw an opportunity to expand distribution with an investment in a California lubricants distributor, and Panama Lubricants Company began distribution of the Germania/Penn Refining lubricants on the West Coast under the brand name Panama. Although the oils were of the finest quality, neither the Merit nor Panama brand names called attention to the fact that these were Pennsylvania-grade lubricants. To resolve this problem, the brand name Pennzoil was chosen in 1916 and gained such acceptance in the marketplace that in 1921 the Oil City Oil and Grease Company became the Pennzoil Company (A

Dynamic art-deco Pennzoil/Pennzip station prototype with illuminated glass block construction. Mt. Lebanon, Pennsylvania, 1941.

Pennsylvania Corporation), while Panama Lubricants Company became the Pennzoil Company (A California Corporation). Meanwhile, Germania and Penn Refining had merged in 1914 and had taken the name Penn-American Refining Company during World War I in response to anti-German sentiment. During this time, the new Penn American remained separate from the Oil

A Pennzoil oil cabinet globe from the 1920s.

City and Panama firms, though Penn American supplied virtually all of their refined product. Ownership of the various firms, too, remained in the hands of several groups of partners, though everyone was not involved in each of the firms. The complex ownership and supply arrangements were resolved in 1924 when Penn American, Pennzoil (Pennsylvania), Pennzoil (California), and another entity that had been created, Pennzoil (New York), were merged to form simply the Pennzoil Company. Pennzoil (New York) marked a significant change in direction for the Pennzoil companies, in that it was established as a gasoline

Pennzoil adopted the Pennzip brand name for gasolines in the mid-1930s.

marketer, operating branded Pennzoil stations in western New York.

In 1921, the Pennzoil Company entered gasoline marketing with branded Pennzoil stations in the Oil City-Titusville area. Formerly, gasoline had been largely a nominal product for Penn American Refining, sold unbranded on the wholesale market. From the Oil City origins, gasoline marketing expanded first into southwestern New York with the establishment of Pennzoil (New York). Next came a network of bulk plants and service stations in eastern Ohio, centered around Cleveland. Meanwhile, lubricants sales were expanded along the West Coast and throughout the East, gradually becoming the national motor oil brand most commonly thought of when a Pennsylvania-grade lubricant was needed.

In the meantime, as Pennzoil developed, South Penn Oil had relatively successful ventures in domestic oil exploration and was becoming a major crude supplier, developing a large number of producing wells in West Virginia. Production was sold on the open market, with an increasing quantity of South Penn crude refined into Pennzoil every year. Indeed, South Penn had become a major supplier to Penn American Refining, and in turn, to the new Pennzoil Companies. As distribution of Pennzoil had grown, the need for a steady source of crude supply for the Pennzoil refinery became a corporate priority. Naturally, South Penn was considered. The timing was fortunate because South Penn had just embarked on a search for steady customers for the increasing production. In 1925, South Penn purchased a 51 percent interest in the Pennzoil Company, with Pennzoil becoming

Pennzip offered an Ethyl-grade product.

a South Penn subsidiary. Pennzoil was now a fully integrated oil company.

Although the Pennzoil gasoline marketing venture was very successful, make no mistake about it, Pennzoil was a lubricants company. With a reliable source of supply, a recently upgraded refinery, and national distribution, Pennzoil in 1930 was poised to become the number-one selling Pennsylvania-grade motor oil brand. To demonstrate the reliability of Pennzoil lubricants, Pennzoil products were made available on racing circuits, from dirt

Curb signs have always been used to promote Pennzoil products. Shown here is a 1920s version.

tracks all the way to Indianapolis. Pennzoil proved to be a winner, as the racing victories began adding up. Every endurance claim was advertised nationally in magazines of the day, and after sealed motor oil containers were introduced about 1934, these claims appeared with text and graphics on the oil cans themselves.

Pennzoil had been one of the first companies to adopt sealed quart cans for distribution for their motor oils. Prior to this time, Pennzoil, and all other oils, were either sold in cans sealed with a twist-off cap or from bulk bottles. Either method proved susceptible to oil substitution, as cans could easily be refilled, and products of any brand, grade, or oil could be stored in bulk tanks from which bottles were filled. With the adoption of the sealed can, the orange-gold color used on previous containers was changed to a bright yellow. The Pennzoil bell had evolved from golden brown to red, but the trademark Pennzoil remained the same. A 1936 marketing campaign, "Be Oil Wise," saw the adoption of three "wise owls" in conjunction with the Pennzoil logo, and the owls would appear on cans for the next several years.

Also in 1936, Pennzoil gasoline was renamed Pennzip, to allow proper national promotion of the Pennzoil brand as a lubricant, since Pennzip gasoline was available from stations in only Pennsylvania, Ohio, New York, and West Virginia. Joint advertising of the Pennzip and Pennzoil brands promoted them as "partners in power." By this time Pennzoil did enjoy national distribution as one of the most successful of the Pennsylvania grade motor oils nationwide. Pennzip gasoline was largely sold through jobber-supplied stations, although the company did operate a few showcase stations direct in some Pennsylvania markets. In about 1940, a new station prototype was introduced, consisting of a glass block structure with internal illumination that turned the entire building into a showcase for Pennzoil/Pennzip products. In spite of this elaborate station design, Pennzip was certainly the least aggressive gasoline marketer among the Standard descendants, as the company remains to this day.

The company provided aviation fuels and lubricants to the military during World War II, adding important equipment to its refinery outside Oil City in the first major changes to the facility since the late 1920s. South Penn saw a large number of successful oil well completions in the early postwar years, and times were good for the company. Taking advantage of the ever-improving financial condition, South Penn began searching for potential acquisitions. In 1952, South Penn purchased controlling interest in Elk Refining Company in Charleston, West Virginia. Elk, an affiliate of Warren, Pennsylvania-based United Refining, was primarily a lubricants refiner but operated the Keystone stations throughout West Virginia. Then, in 1955, South Penn completed the purchase of Pennzoil, solidifying the alliance that began twenty-five years earlier.

Shortly after the completion of the Pennzoil-South Penn merger, the Pennzip gasoline brand reverted to Pennzoil and became an increasingly important jobber brand in Pennsylvania, Ohio, West Virginia, and New York. Market expansion was underway when, in 1963, South Penn merged with two Gulf Coast crude producers, Zapata and Stetco. The new entity became

A later Pennzoil curb sign from the early 1930s.

Pennzoil Company. Also in 1963, Pennzoil purchased Pennsylvania rival Wolf's Head Refining Company. Wolf's Head, founded as Empire Refining in 1879, marketed a nationally known motor oil and lubricants brand and branded about fifty service stations in Pennsylvania. Later that same year, Pennzoil completed the purchase of Elk Refining, and within two years the Pennzoil brand replaced the Keystone brand on service stations throughout West Virginia and in Kentucky, giving Pennzoil gasoline market penetration from Buffalo, New York, south to Bluefield, Virginia, and Pikeville, Kentucky.

During this era of merger and expansion, the Pennzoil lubricants line grew in product diversity and brand recognition. Wolf's Head oils would continue to this day with a separate product line, as each brand had its own customer appeal and specialized products. Pennzoil continued the South Penn traditions as well, as exploration encompassed a wider area of domestic oil producing regions.

In 1968, Pennzoil merged with United Gas, a Texas-based natural gas production and transportation company. This merger contributed significantly to the diversity of corporate activities. Also in 1968, Pennzoil purchased the Fleet-Wing Corporation, a Sohio subsidiary that operated distribution for another jobber-oriented gasoline marketer. Most of the Fleet-Wing stations would

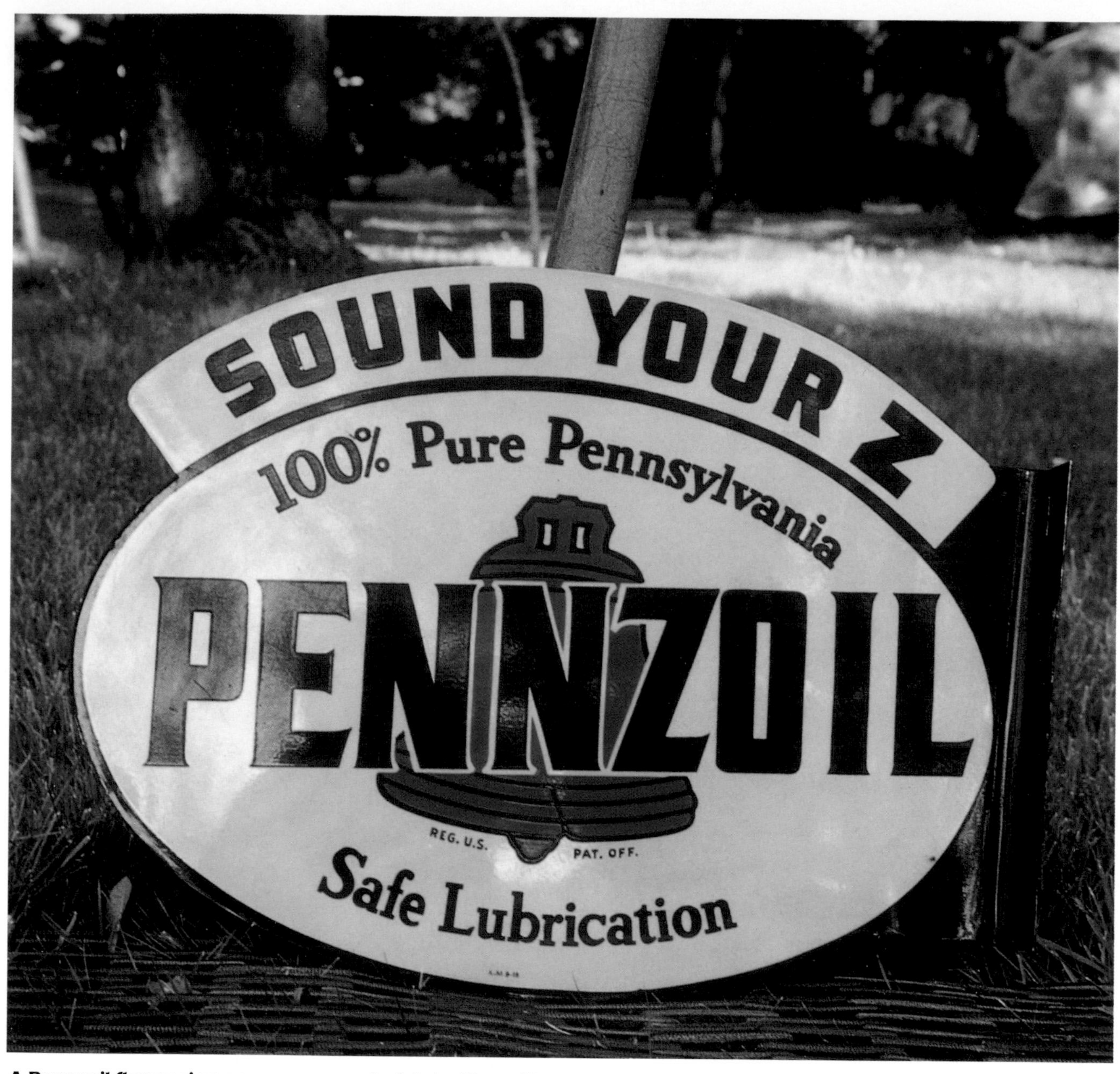

A Pennzoil flange sign encourages motorists to "Sound Your Z."

rebrand to Pennzoil within five years, although several jobbers keep the brand alive to this day.

In 1973, Pennzoil made another significant purchase, that of Pennsylvania Refining Company. Pennsylvania Refining, better known as Pennreco, operated the Penn-Drake and Pennreco service stations in Pennsylvania and marketed the Penn Drake motor oil line. Founded in 1878, Pennreco remains a Pennzoil operation and significant producer of specialty lubricants to this day.

Without a far-flung network of gasoline stations to support, Pennzoil weathered the gas shortages of the 1970s in better shape than most. Stations were virtually 100 percent jobber owned, and supply problems could be dealt with on an exchange basis with other suppliers. Profits from Pennzoil lubricants could carry the company through tough times, as well.

Pennzoil made the headlines again in 1984 when it agreed to merge with Getty Oil. With significant production and marketing

Pennzoil signage appeared on garages selling Pennzoil lubricants in the 1930s.

throughout the Northeast under the Getty brand and in the Midwest under the Skelly name, the merger was significant for both companies. Two days after the agreement was made, Texaco stepped in and purchased Getty from other stockholders in a very complex transaction. Pennzoil, in turn, sued Texaco for interfering with Pennzoil's acquisition plans. Four years of court battles ensued before Texaco settled, paying more than $3 billion, in a move that broke Texaco apart. Pennzoil overwhelmed with cash, wisely invested heavily in exploration and refining assets to solidify its position as America's premier lubricants manufacturer.

In the early 1990s, Pennzoil began expanding its gasoline marketing base, signing on jobbers in those areas of Virginia and Tennessee that could be supplied with existing facilities. Currently, the Pennzoil brand appears on nearly 1,000 stations in seven states. The corporation, with nearly $5 billion in assets, ranks seventeenth in assets among major oil companies and is in twenty-fifth place in number of retail locations, making it the smallest gasoline marketer among the surviving Standard companies.

Assorted Pennzoil cans from the 1930s touts particular features of Pennzoil products.

The Other Standard Descendants

The 1911 Supreme Court breakup of Standard Oil created thirty-four separate entities. Standard's net worth of $660 million at the time of the breakup has been surpassed by each of the nine surviving marketing companies detailed in this history, plus several others listed below. These nine were chosen because they are the surviving gasoline marketers, familiar images to the motoring public. But what of the other Standard descendants? Do they survive? Most do, in some form, merged with their former siblings. A few have merged with non-Standard entities until their heritage and identity have been lost. The following chart lists all thirty-four companies and their status at the time of this writing.

1. Standard Oil Company of New Jersey is now Exxon Corporation.
2. Standard Oil Company of New York is now Mobil Corporation.
3. Standard Oil Company of Indiana is now Amoco Corporation.
4. Standard Oil Company of California is now Chevron Corporation.
5. Standard Oil Company of Ohio is now BP America.
6. The Ohio Oil Company is now Marathon Oil, a subsidiary of USX, Inc.
7. The Atlantic Refining Company is now Atlantic Richfield Company.
8. Continental Oil Company is now Conoco, Inc., a subsidiary of DuPont Corporation.
9. South Penn Oil Company is now Pennzoil, Inc.
10. Borne, Scrymser Company survives today as Borne Chemical.
11. Cheesebrough Manufacturing survives today as Cheesebrough-Pond's, Inc., manufacturers of Vaseline products.
12. Washington Oil Company survives as a Pennsylvania oil production firm.
13. Union Tank Car Company survives as a petroleum transportation firm.
14. Buckeye Pipe Line Company survives as a common carrier pipeline today.
15. Vacuum Oil Company merged with Standard of New York in 1931.
16. Standard Oil Company of Nebraska merged with Standard of Indiana in 1939.
17. Standard Oil Company of Kansas merged with Standard of Indiana in 1948.
18. Standard Oil Company of Kentucky merged with Standard of California in 1961.
19. Colonial Oil Company merged with Beacon Oil in 1928 and the combined entity, Colonial Beacon, merged with Standard of New Jersey in 1931.
20. Solar Refining merged with Standard of Ohio in 1931.
21. Anglo-American Oil Company merged with Standard of New Jersey in 1930.
22. Waters Pierce Oil Company became Pierce Petroleum before merging with Sinclair Oil in 1930.

23. Prairie Oil and Gas merged with Sinclair Oil in 1932.

24. Galena-Signal Oil Company merged with Valvoline Oil Company in 1932.

25. Indiana Pipe Line merged with Buckeye Pipe Line in 1942.

26. Northern Pipeline merged with Buckeye Pipe Line in 1964.

27. New York Transit merged with Buckeye Pipe Line in 1964.

28. South-West Pennsylvania Pipelines merged with National Transit in 1952.

29. National Transit merged with South Penn Oil Company in 1965.

30. Eureka Pipe Line merged with South Penn Oil Company in 1947.

31. Cumberland Pipe Line merged with Ashland Oil in 1931.

32. Southern Pipeline merged with Ashland Oil in 1949.

33. Crescent Pipe Line did not survive the Great Depression.

34. Swan and Finch survived as an industrial lubricants manufacturer until the 1960s.

As you can see, Standard descendants tended to form alliances with their former siblings. Only Sinclair, with close ties to Standard of Indiana, and Ashland/Valvoline, with close ties to Standard of Ohio, have had any significant relationships with the Standard descendants. Of the thirty-four companies, only two appear to have completely liquidated. It is likely that Standard descendants acquired assets of these companies as well, but that cannot be determined at this time.

And the threat of monopolization of America's petroleum industry, so deftly eliminated by the government in 1911, was hardly a threat at all. Many of the Standard siblings have long since surpassed the parent company in assets and net worth. Indeed, the petroleum industry, even the entire twentieth century, would have been different had there been no Standard. Standard was the fuel—and the lubricant—for the industrialization in the nineteenth century and the mobilization in the twentieth century of the world.

Index